# Living Life
# Outside The Box

## by
## Gene Hoff

I

ISBN: 1-4208-5506-9 (sc)

Library of Congress Control Number: 2005906034


Printed in the United States of America

ISBN 1-4208-5506-9
90000

9 781420 855067

# Disclaimer:

There are periods in any life which are routine and unremarkable and such there are in mine. While writing this account of my seventy four years, I have relied entirely on my memory and included only those parts which I think have a story to tell. The interesting thing about memory is there is no way of knowing if we are remembering things as they really happened or do we only remember remembering how they happened. As this is a story about my impressions of events; my memory of them is what is germane. My only problem now is I keep forgetting I can't remember things. So any distortions, omissions, or inaccuracies are unintentional and should be forgiven.

# Table of Contents

# Chapter One   Stories Usually Start Here

I take computer in hand to record the story of my seventy five year long life. Who am I you ask? Ill tell you. I am not a famous lawyer or politician or movie star. I am nobody. If a worldwide contest for the most nobody were held, I would be right up there with the runners up. I would like to claim I am the world's champion nobody but being modest; I don't want to brag about myself too much.

So where to begin? I suppose at the beginning.

I lived the first eighteen years of my life on a farm in the northwest corner of Ohio. Ours was, I believe, a typical rural environment common during the Great Depression of the 30's and the war years of the 40's. Like many others at that time, we were poor but I didn't know it. Living with my Father, Mother, Grandmother, and siblings on our farm, we always had the necessities of life but very few of the luxuries. My first eighteen years were quite unremarkable actually and typical of rural life at that time but if you are consumed with curiosity; you can read all about them in Chapters Seven, Eight, Nine, and Ten.

My life was pretty typical for that of a chattel slave. When I wasn't in school, I was working on our farm. I would plow the fields, plant the seeds, hoe the weeds, pick the pickles and tomatoes, husk the corn, milk the cows, feed the chickens, feed the pigs, shovel cow manure, shovel chicken leavings, and in the end, I ran away from home and joined the Navy.

Yea, you heard me. I ran away from home and joined the Navy. Well actually, I ran away from home to join the Air Force but their recruiting office in Toledo was closed the day I arrived so instead of waiting for them to open, I just went next door and joined the Navy. This was June 6, 1949 and I had just turned eighteen one month earlier.

The next day found me aboard the train headed for Boot Camp at Glenview Ill. Let me tell you riding on that train was a new experience for me. I was thrown in with a bunch of big city hoods and my profane vocabulary was expanded well beyond the familiar "Damn", "Hell" and another incomprehensible expression my Father used which had something to do with a male chicken.

I stupidly expected this Navy thing would be a big improvement in my life but boy was I fooled. On my first day there, they stole all my hair and replaced my clothes with an unkempt issue designed to totally obliterate any sense of individuality I might have had.

I don't know the reason behind it but the Navy has an absolute abhorrence of anything pleasurable. It is designed to make life miserable and this design works. My life became a blur of classes, marching, inspections, and watches without end. I marched everywhere I went. I marched to chow. I marched to class. I marched to get my immune shots. I marched to the drill field to do exercises to dissipate the pain of getting the shots.

I found the most difficult part of this life was the unnatural hours they expected me to keep. Whoever came up with the idea that one should arise at six o'clock while its still night and be ready to go back to bed by nine o'clock in the afternoon? These hours were, in my estimation, at least four hours to soon. One should sleep until ten o'clock when it's finally morning and retire at one o'clock at night after all the bars close.

The Navy however had its own way of imposing its ideas on me and unhappily it always prevailed in this matter.

Another quirky obsession is its insistence on uniforms being spotlessly clean at all times. To that end they made the summer uniform bright white so as to make the smallest innocent violation easily detectable.

After three months of this unhappy incarceration, I was finally released for a short leave of absents. I flew for the first time in my life and headed back to Toledo to join my intended.

Hold it! Where did this "my intended" come from you ask?

Well if you must know, this is how that all came about.

Back in my slave days, I had met Sharon; a curvaceous red headed young lady who didn't have enough sense to run screaming when she first met me. I was able to overwhelm her with my charm and my father's new 1948 Kaiser.

(For you younger readers this was a short lived Automobile Brand which disappeared after 1955) I was seventeen at the time and my view of the world was greatly distorted by having to peer out from behind a gigantic psychological phallus. (A Ten Dollar word for use in polite company) This condition is caused by a quirk of nature which creates a strange inverse proportion of blood that can exist between a male's groin and his brain. The more blood there is in one location, the less there is in the other. At that age, I was not able to distinguish the difference, if there is one, between being horny and being in love. I must confess my sole motive was to get laid as soon and as often as possible. Not having completely overthrown all the moral imperatives taught by my mother, I believed the only honorable way I could archive my goal was to be married. Later I came to realize that was not the most honorable way of doing it.

All my sexual experiences to this point had been self inflicted and I was in no mood to make this a permanent condition.

Hang on and I'll get back to flying to Toledo in a bit but first, let me explain about this self inflicted thing.

I can't answer for my two younger brothers but I know I was very lucky to have accidentally discovered the joy of masturbation long before I knew what the thing was designed for. Now I don't want you the think this was practiced to the exclusion of all other kinds of play. However I certainty didn't think there was anything wrong with it except, for modesty, should only be practiced in private. One must think of something when doing it and I chose to imagine soft furry animals. I guess I had the soft furry part right but I was just  misdirected.

Now lets get back to where we were flying to Toledo.

Sharon was staying with a friend and I didn't tell her what time I would be arriving so it could be a big surprise when I walked in. I asked the taxi driver to let me out in the ally behind their house but then he ratted on me by driving around to the front where everyone was waiting and told them where I was.

Boy was it good to be back with her. My only contact with her for the last three months had been by mail. We were both smokers and she always included with her letter, a single lipstick stained cigarette. Even though it was flattened, I still enjoyed it.

My having a weeks leave and not wanting to be separated again, we decided to get married right away and drove over the boarder into Kentucky and took advantage of the "Quickie Marriage" industry which flourished there.

Now assigned to the Navel Air Training Center in Memphis Tennessee, Sharon and I set-up housekeeping in a small one room apartment over a garage in the suburbs of Memphis and I started a routine which would span the next nine months. I was spending my days going to school and my nights in the sack with Sharon. All this activity in the sack generally has a predictable outcome and in spite of our precautions, of course Sharon became pregnant.

Considering my poor academic record in High School, (this is explained in depth in Chapter Nine) it would seem I would have had a similar experience here at the Navel Training Center but this time it was very different. What I learned here, I would use in one form or another for my entire life. I came out of this phase with a basic understanding of Hydraulics, Pneumatics, Electronics, Metallurgy, and Meteorology.

I was next assigned to FASRON 104 in Pawtuxet Md where things got really boring. You can thank me for leaving out all the dull details of this next six months duty.

My story now picks up with me aboard the troop ship H J Hodges on my way to Port Lyote, French Morocco.

Ah Ha! Now this is getting better.

Sharon had given birth to our son, Terry Lynn, three months earlier and had returned to Ohio to live with her parents during my overseas assignment.

This was my first ocean voyage and the trip on this small troop transport was no pleasure cruise featuring an "All you can eat Buffet" with Shuffleboard on the deck later. It was more like "All the greasy pork chops and gravy you can gag down while seasick" with a crooked Poker or Crap game below decks later. The only diversions I had were losing my money in one of those games or watching the female dependent passengers exercising on the restricted deck above us. Female fraternization with us lowlifes on the ship was absolutely forbidden.

I will never understand why human males will voluntarily put themselves in all kinds of "look but don't touch" situations and call that fun. It's that blood deprivation to the brain thing again I think.

Twelve long days later I was very glad to see the sand tan outline of Casablanca appear on the horizon.

The Buss ride from Casablanca to Port Lyote wound along the coast through many small Arab settlements; the sights and smells of which did much to dispel the lingering musty aura of the ship.

Surveying my options after I arrived, I discovered there were as many men leaving as there were arriving which created a buyers market for all the things the departing troops couldn't take with them. With only a limited amount of money, I had to choose between an apartment in town with a full time live in female companion or a 1941 Packard convertible coupe.

I choose the convertible.

Well this car wasn't really a convertible because the cloth top had long ago rotted away. The engine had thrown a rod straight through the block and both front fenders displayed the scars of multiple losing encounters with inflexible opponents. It however fit right in with my view of things. I did, after a while, make a cloth top but as I didn't have the original framework, I was unable to make it truly convertible. That was only a temporary condition though. One night while cruising in the moonlight, I got carried away by the moment and reconverted it to its original topless condition.

Well anyway, thereafter that car and I were occasionally good for a laugh when driving through the Base front gate with no top and the windshield wipers franticly oscillating in the driving rain.

It didn't take me long to have enough of this celibacy nonsense so I made an application with the Navy to have Sharon and Terry join me here in Africa.

Getting ready for her arrival, I rented a small house a few miles off the Base on the beach. Built on a sand dune, its foundation had shifted and the front was down a few inches lower than the back. Anything dropped on the floor would end up against the front wall. Across this front, two large windows without glass faced the ocean and when their solid wooden shutters were closed in bad weather, the room became as dark as night. The only other features in the house were one small bedroom, a kitchen and a toilet. Contrasting with the two hole (No waiting) outhouse I frequently shared with my kid sister back on the farm, here the toilet was the sole fixture in its own small closet size room.

Now you are probably wondering what I was doing with my sister in the outhouse on our farm.

Well I'll tell you.

Only a year apart, we were like twins and completely innocent and uninhibited with each other. We frequently would find ourselves far from the house working in the fields when nature called and with nowhere to hide even if we thought we should; we were left with no choice but to do business where we were. So naturally at other times we would frequently share the outhouse. Never having been told this was shameful; we naturally didn't think it was. I didn't think her looking different than me was strange. That was just how girls looked. It was easy to distinguish them from boys because they had long hair, wore dresses, and they always needed to squat when they peed.

Now I have to jerk you back to my house in Morocco.

Oh! To Hell with the house. Let's get to something more interesting.

A welcome break in our normal routine here in Morocco was an occasional assignment to TAD (temporary additional duty). I was still waiting for Sharon's arrival and when my turn for this duty came, I welcomed being assigned for a couple of weeks on the island of Malta. The unit here was a small crew whose only function was to be on call and available if a transit aircraft needed an emergency repair.

My days here soon slipped into a predictable pattern. Starting in the afternoon, I would drive my rented Morris Minor into the largest city, Valetta, and hang out on its most infamous street we called "The Gut." This was a long street on an incline lined on both sides with bars full of B Girls. Anyone who attempted to make it from one end of this street to the other, had a night's work ahead of him. It took a strong will to get back in the barracks in time for a few hours sleep.

The military has no mercy when it comes to reveille so at six AM, barely awake, I would stagger down to the street below where the local dairyman is selling cold milk by the glass.

Sipping the milk with shaking hands, I would reluctantly fall in for muster. The next few hours were spent at the flight line in a semiconscious state. Luckily there were no emergencies which needed my attention. At about three in the afternoon, I would feel human enough to have a shower and then with some of the guys, head for a small nameless hotel where we would get our daily meal of steak and eggs. Because our food was cooked on a single charcoal brazier, it would not be ready for at least three or four Heineken beers. Time here was measured in beer. After eating, it's back to the Gut to do it all over again. Luckily, I had only a two week tour or I might not have survived to tell the tale.

Back in Morocco, I was now in charge of the Battery Locker. This was fortunate for me as an unusual condition developed which was unexpected to say the least.

Because of their frequent visits with the civilian population, the crew would regularly suffer from an infestation of body lice. More commonly known as "crabs", this affliction would sweep through like a plague.

So this time when I was blamelessly stricken, I didn't know what I had. By the time I did, the matter had gotten nearly out of control. I went to sickbay and they gave me some kind of powder to apply. I tried their method but after one day, I didn't seem to be getting any positive results. The evening of the second day I decided to literally take matters into my own hands and came up with a kill or cure remedy. I had available to me the one compound, sulfuric acid, which I hoped would work. I knew it was caustic on cloth and flesh alike so I reasoned it would be fatal to these lice.

Be warned the following paragraph is graphic so you might want to turn away for the next few sentences.

While holding one handful of acid neutralizing soda at the ready, I applied the acid to my affected areas with a small brush. Waiting as long as I could while the acid did its work, I judged the time by how warm things were getting. Then after a generous application of the neutralizing soda and a hot shower, everything was back to normal.

You can resume reading here.

This method, though highly effective, is not to be recommended for general use and I disclaim any responsibility for any damage resulting from it.

Another time, I was one of a group who had an opportunity to visit the city of Meknes. We visited the area in the city where Moroccan leather was made. This leather has a distinct odor perhaps due to the fact that sheep urine is one of the primary elements in the Tanning process. The people involved in this activity reportedly never leave their area as the odor they carry made them unwelcome in polite society. The only part of this process which was not made clear to me was how they went about collecting the Sheep's urine. How does one go about doing that? Do you suppose they really run around holding a bucket behind a sheep?

Now here is the good part.

Another unrelated but very interesting stop was a visit to an area called White City. This was a government controlled walled enclave which housed dozens of young women working as prostitutes. As we entered the front gate, we were descended upon by a horde of girls trying to pull us into their respective establishments. We were told ahead of time, if we didn't remove everything loose like watches, pens, and jewelry, it would be deftly removed and stolen by the swarming inhabitants of this place. It was my understanding, that most of the Arab females in there were working off debts incurred by their families and as far as I could see, all but one of the many establishments were filled with these Arab women. The sole exception was one house which featured only French girls.

I felt no one should have to live like that but strangely enough, most of the girls I talked to seemed to be quite happy. Judged by the apparent disproportional ratio of customers to girls, it would seem they were not terribly overworked.

I spent most of the night in the bar of the French section talking to the girls there. I had acquired a limited amount of

Bordello French from the locals in Port Lyote and with the help of some of the English speaking girls, I was able have some semblance of a conversation. The typical accommodations offered here were of two types. One was what was called a "Quickie" which is self explanatory and the other was an "Over Nighter" which is also self explanatory. Suffice to say, shame on me, I was awakened in the morning by a male servant bringing coffee and French pastries to my room.

The next day we visited an excavated ancient Roman city. I found this place strangely attractive. To be able to see and touch a stone that had been formed and placed over a thousand years ago gave me a strong mystic feeling. I could feel what it must have been like in those narrow streets and alleys all those years ago. Maybe I had seen too many Movies set in similar places.

Much had not changed in Africa from the early Roman days. Some places in the native quarters are much the same as they were a thousand years ago. I once observed an old woman in an alley squatting in front of a small charcoal braiser on which she was cooking a completely intact sheep's head. Hide, hair, horns and all were still attached and I suppose it was easier to extract the edible parts if they were first cooked in their original container.

As the Navy does not have a Military Police division, these police duties, known as Shore Patrol, are filled by ordinary seamen on temporary assignment.

I had the good fortune at one time to be assigned to this duty and this greatly improved my outlook on being in the service. Many privileges came with this job and there were no demands on my time outside of my Watch. Our main tasks were keeping order in town and hauling in drunken sailors from the local brothels. We sometimes were accompanied by US Marine MPs or French Gendarmes but generally were on patrol alone.

The best duty on this beat was in the nearby city of Rabat and for safety reasons, we always patrolled in pairs. We would routinely inspect the houses of ill repute looking for American servicemen and one place in particular was always the most fun.

Our visit would start with a knock on the establishment's door. A small window would open. Two eyes peer out at us.

Small window closes. We hear a series of short hand claps.

A moment later the main door opens and we enter a building with a large central courtyard surrounded by many doors leading to private rooms. One or two girls with three or more drinks each are sitting at the dozen or so small tables scattered about. Apparently these girls were heavy drinkers. Well obviously, there had been many men sitting with them only moments earlier. We are ushered into one of the private rooms and couple of "Very Friendly Girls" bring in a tray of thick French bread sandwiches and strong Turkish coffee. I found eating with a girl sitting on my lap gave a whole new meaning to the expression "Elegant Dining." When we are ready to depart, our hosts first leave us and again we hear the hand clapping signal and in spite of our true diligence, we were never able to find a single American service man in that establishment.

I never could understand why the military publicly was so anti-prostitution when privately, it was so universally embraced.

The French Gendarmes shared their offices in town with us and I was able to observe a great disparity between our police actions and theirs. One day I witnessed a young woman lying on the bare tile floor being prodded by one of the Gendarmes with his night stick. She obviously was under the influence of something and she was growling and snapping back at him like a teased dog. I really felt sorry for her and wanted to do something but this was not our jurisdiction and as guests in their country, we were instructed to never interfere with any French Police actions. The Gendarme only laughingly said "Too much zig zig." I could only draw my own conclusions about what that meant.

After only six months of this good duty, I was reluctantly again back in the electric shop.

After six months of waiting, Sharon and Terry finally joined me in Port Lyote. They came in on the bus from Casablanca in the afternoon and as it had been a long hard trip for her with the baby, I immediately drove them out to my house on the beach.

Poor thing didn't get much rest however as we were soon joined by three of my friends from the electric shop. The stated reason for their visit was to meet my wife and son but the real reason was to delay as long as possible, any romantic notions I might have. I had a host of friends.

I was very happy to have her and Terry with me again and we settled in and life became routine. I went to the Base every day and Sharon played housewife. Looking back now I wonder what she did all day while I was on the base. The only entertainment available was Armed Forces Radio and an occasional movie on the Base. Living right on the beach made swimming readily available but even though we were in a hot desert region, the ocean water was quite cold.

We were very lucky one day when I happened to be at home when a small emergency occurred. Terry was playing in front of the house where a stone wall with steps separated our yard from the street and he somehow fell and hit his mouth on these stones. I found him crying loudly with blood streaming out of his mouth and it appeared to me he had knocked out his two front teeth. I immediately drove him to the infirmary on the Base and after the doctor examined him, he told us Terry's teeth had not been knocked out but had been driven up inside his gums.

Miraculously these teeth, over time, descended back down into their original position.

Except for the small dog that would routinely hump our legs on the flight line and an aircraft that caught on fire while I was starting it, I can't think of a single interesting thing that happened for the next year. As an old married man, my adventurous spirit was contained a good deal.

A year after joining me here in Africa, Sharon gave birth to our second son, Jerry Lesley. Apparently I still hadn't figured out what caused that.

A normal tour with dependence over seas was three years and at the end of that time, I was assigned to the U. S. Reserve Training Station in Squantum Mass.

Sharon and I, with the kids, hitched a ride sitting on cargo sacks in a Mats (Military Air Transport) plane back to the United States and landed in the snow in Squantum Mass. After three years in the warmth of Africa, the cold here was quite a shock

The station here was a reserve training base and I was sent to instructor training school. Back in the squadron after graduating, I was overcome by a terribly depression.

Looking back it is hard to explain but at that time maybe it was the realization that I had left a life of limited options and choices on the farm only to end up in another which was even more restricted. At one time I even fantasized faking my death and changing my name and starting all over. I cannot explain it adequately, even to myself. I even consulted a Navy Psychiatrist who didn't seem to have any answers either. Needless to say my state of mind destroyed my marriage and Sharon moved with the boys back to Ohio. She was in no way responsible for my condition. She had always been a supportive and loving wife and had done everything she possibly could but I was completely consumed with despair. Luckily, Sharon was an only child so she could live for a while with her parents. She subsequently remarried and her husband adopted our two boys. I took the arguable position that a part time second father was not the best thing for them, so I stayed out of their life.

I am still haunted by the images in my mind of that time. It is as though I was two entities occupying the same body. One of us wanted to stay and do the right thing but the other one was forcing me to go. I think this was the tearing apart of the part of me formed in my childhood which had a strict code of what was the proper way to live and the part of me that needed to be free from them.

Also at that time I made a decision which would turn out to be one of the smartest I ever made. I did not plan to be celibate for the rest of my life and as I didn't think it would be a good idea to have any more children, I set about arranging a vasectomy. I was twenty two years old when I had this surgery and I never have had one second of regret.

Now like in the movies.

Scene fadeout.

# Chapter Two   Some Years Later

Scene fade-in.

Twenty three years have passed.

Picture this. I am sitting on the deck of my sailboat anchored next to the fisherman's pier in Santa Cruz California. I had decided to sail to Hawaii and I am anxiously waiting to see if the cute young lady I had earlier recruited as a crew was going to show up.

Hold it you say. How in the world did I get here?

OK, Ok I'll back up a bit.

Let's see, I guess a good place to start would be back when I was living in Dallas, Texas.

(If you must know how I got there, insert Chapter Eleven here. Otherwise the following is the short version.)

I had frittered away ten years here in Texas working in the newly emerging Integrated Circuit Industry. Somewhere in that time, my younger brother Richard showed up on my doorstep.

After serving eleven years in the Air Force Band, he had decided to live with his older brother for a while.

Then one day for reasons which escape me, I had a sudden inexplicable thought and told a friend "I think I'll build a boat and sail around the world." This idea was like a religious conversion. From that moment on, I devoted all my spare energies to that single end.

The first thing I had to decide on was what kind of a boat to build. I knew of course it had to be a sailboat. After studying all the different designs available, it became clear to me that I wanted something unique. I would have to come up with my own design and I did this by not following convention but instead, combined engineering with art on the project.

At a point where I had nearly finished the designing phase I started getting a little worried about where I could start building. As Dallas is not exactly on the ocean, I knew I would have to move to a more favorable location. Now, as it would many times in the future, fate stepped in and gave me a hand.

Clark Davis, an engineer I had previously worked with at Texas Instruments, called late one night and asked, "How would you like to work at National Semiconductor in sunny Santa Clara, California?" I had no idea where Santa Clara was and I asked "Is it close to water?" His "Yup" was all I needed.

Richard and I loaded our gear in his Volvo and headed west. Taking turns driving, we arrived in Santa Clara in the late afternoon two days later. Stopping at the first Motel we came to after leaving the Freeway, we had no idea we were only about two miles from my new employer.

The next morning, Richard dropped me off at National and set about finding us a place to live. He stopped at a small restaurant nearby and as the result of talking with its young proprietor; was given directions to a small settlement only four miles up the road and right on San Francisco Bay.

By the time Richard picked me up after work that afternoon, he had managed to survey the layout in this little town called Alviso and had rented a two bedroom house trailer next to a boat building yard about a hundred yards from the water.

I immediately rented the back portion of the building next to our trailer and got started building my boat.

(See the Appendix A for a detailed description and pictures of the boat's construction)

Located at the very bottom of San Francisco Bay, Alviso was a one of a kind place. To begin with, the entire town which had originally been a thriving port exporting hides, tallow, and grain was now a back water residential area occupied primarily by Mexican Americans. Because of silting from agriculture, the four mile long slough connecting Alviso to the Bay was now only usable by small pleasure and fishing craft. Additionally, the entire area had subsided fifteen feet from its original height making it prone to flooding.

The San Jose-San Francisco railroad ran through the western edge of town, cutting off a small slice of land bordering the slough where a lot of amateur boat building flourished. The long abandoned main building of the Bayside Cannery dominated this location and provided space for much of this activity. One of the many facilities in this building was the communally available shower.

One day while waiting my turn for a bath outside by the door, I became aware of low moans and heavy breathing coming from the shower's interior. My understandable reaction was; God, I sure hope that person isn't in there alone.

There is something about owning a boat that tugs at the psyche of many men. Obviously a boat is a common physical representation of freedom, romance, and adventure. I know when a commercial attempts to promote a picture of success; they often depict the lucky recipient in a boat sailing off into the wide blue sea. So it's easy to understand what motivates us.

Each boat building project here had a unique story connected with it and there were as many characters as there were boats.

One poor soul working on a large Trimaran, expressed his intention of sailing to Tahiti when he finished. The fact he was suffering from acute emphysema and had to frequently use a motorized ventilating device to aid his breathing didn't seem to diminish his optimism. This kind of attitude always reminded me of a Stan Freberg skit where the expression, "Everyone must have a Dream." was used so effectively. Without a dream, there would have been no adventurers and explorers throughout the ages.

Another character here was a young East Germany immigrant who was in the process of welding together a wire frame for a thirty five foot ferro-cement sailboat. This method of constructing displacement hulls was fairly common at that time so this didn't seem too strange. He had a different way of eating hot dogs that I often copied. Simply dipping a plain wiener into the mustard jar and biting off the flavored end was all that was required. Who said it is necessary to eat bread with everything.

Then there was another dreamer who was building a machine shop in the forward part of his Trimaran with the expectations of supporting himself as a machinist while sailing around the world.

A sheet of plywood with other assorted pieces of drift wood attached to two empty oil drums was the floating home for our local representative of the homeless. Shoeless and un-bathed in all weather, he presented a calm unshaven earth colored persona to this world.

Another character who wore Kilts most of the time was my neighbor for awhile. He was married but I never saw his wife. The small TV in his boat was always turned on as he said it was like having another person keeping company with him. His boat was an older wooden motor launch and I heard years later he had left San Francisco heading for Portland and was never heard from again. Either he was lost at sea or he simply didn't think it was important to stay in touch.

This place also had another tragic story to tell. A young man I knew very well had acquired the unassembled fiberglass hull and deck of a Trimaran Kit boat. These two parts were designed for two slightly different size boats and a lot of improvising was needed to get them joined together. I don't know however if this fact had anything to do with the ensuing disaster. He and his fiancée had gone sailing beyond the Golden Gate when a large wave capsized their boat. He was able to swim free but his fiancée was trapped inside and by the time the Coast Guard got to them and affected a rescue, she had drowned. This greatly saddened me as they had been living in a small room off the larger room I was using and I usually saw them every day. There is always a great sadness connected with the senseless untimely death a young person.

Limited to working only evenings and weekends on the boat, my progress was additionally hampered by the frequent inclement weather enjoyed by the Bay area in winter. I did what I could as opportunity presented itself. At one time, there was six inches of rain water on the floor of my work space. I tried to drain the water away by cutting groves in the road connecting the potholes so the water could flow into the gutter on the opposite side of the street next to me but this got me into trouble with the authorities. Picky picky these people. Getting across the muddy area between the road and our trailer also presented a challenge. At various times we placed old boards in a zigzag pattern on the low wet spots between the higher grassy islands giving us a reasonably mud free escape route.

For transportation at that time, I purchased a Honda 90 motorcycle. The first day I took it out on the back road leading out of town and opened her up to see how fast it would go.

Having no previous experience on motorcycles, I chickened out at about thirty five miles an hour. I rode it to work every day and sometimes took much longer trips to San Francisco. Things were much simpler in those days. When it rained, I would make a rain-coat by simply cutting three holes in a large plastic garbage bag and pull it over my head. Having only a motorcycle presented some real challenges when it came to hauling supplies for the boat construction. This was made somewhat easier when later; I bought a larger Honda 175. Perhaps I made a record of some sort when I managed to carry on that motorcycle, a 4 by 8 sheet of plywood two miles from the lumber yard to the boat.

This was the middle of the "Hippy" age and I enthusiastically joined up with the movement. My transportation was exclusively motorcycles. In the winter I wore a fringed sleeved split cowhide leather jacket tied together in front with a small rope. Open toed leather slippers with cotton stuffed in my ears to ward off an ear ache completed my usual wardrobe. Somewhere in there I also stopped shaving and getting my hair cut. I thereafter sported a full beard in front with a long ponytail in the back.

To fill the time when I couldn't work on the boat, my brother Richard and I formed a small musical group we called The Casual Two. The name is self explanatory as there was only two of us in it. Richard would play our portable electronic organ with one hand and reach across and play our vibraphone with the other. I had modified the tuning of my electric guitar which allowed me to play the base line with my thumb on the two low strings and piano chords with my fingers on the top four high strings. This and a simple drum beat with my foot on a tambourine completed our sound.

We would play at any opportunity without charge. More often than not, our only gratuity was all the booze we could drink. We didn't care as performing was payment enough. This though, could sometimes add a bit of drama as one morning after a performance, we could not remember who had driven home the previous night. I don't thing drinking impaired our driving; only our memory.

With the maturity of old age I can look back at this as being pretty irresponsible but again, I guess sometimes it's better to be lucky than smart.

Eventually we started writing and arranging our own songs. Discouraged by the limit of having only two bodies performing, I bought a four channel quadraphonic tape deck and rebuilt it into a four channel recorder which we could use to layer as many tracks of recording as we desired. Using this device we created arrangements including Six Voices with, Base, Piano, Drums, and Guitar accompaniment. With the ever present help of cigarettes and red wine coolers, we spent hour after hour into the night arranging and recording our music.

There was one other happening in this time period which I suppose I should mention. Being still young and healthy, I saw no advantage in remaining celibate so when an opportunity to change that condition presented itself, I could hardly refuse. I was having an affair with a married lady who was permanently separated from her husband. I naturally thought her condition would protect me from doing something stupid.

BEEEEP! Wrong again. The clever thing got a divorce and before I knew it I was married again. She knew from the start I was building my boat and that I planned on sailing off when it was finished. She also had no intention of joining me on my adventure. No great love affair but ours was none the less a pleasant and satisfying relationship.

Time has a way of slipping by when you have a lot of activities going and it did slip by.

Finally in April, 1976, I had the boat ready to try sailing. The name "Flying Sorceress", I chose for the boat was fitting because its appearance was that of a flying saucer with two banana shaped hulls suspended from beneath on each side. Its design was completely different than anything anyone had ever seen. The interior was quite roomy, having two double berths with a head (nautical term for toilet) on each side and a central galley and saloon extending forward from the main hatch.

I had decided on Hawaii as the first place I wanted to visit but first I had to get out of Alviso. At high tide, Richard and I motored down the muddy slough and into San Francisco Bay.

The fading light of evening forced us to anchor in a small

bay next to San Francisco's sport stadium, Candlestick Park.

A dense fog that had formed during the night delayed our departure until nearly noon the next day. Finally under way, we motored under the Bay Bridge and anchored in Aquatic Park at the foot of fisherman's wharf. I had earlier acquired a small solid Styrofoam kayak type boat to be used to commute between my boat and the shore and here, we gave it a try for the first time. After going ashore and doing a little shopping, we attempted to get our supplies with us in the little boat. This only resulted in it tipping over two times before we finally succeeded in getting back on board. That little boat was so light and unstable, it was nearly unusable and I knew I would unquestionably have to acquire a better one for getting to shore and back.

The next morning, after sailing across the bay to Sausalito, I tied up to the buoy off the sea-wall by Olson's Restaurant and put Richard ashore.

My first order of business now was to get a new dinghy. Sausalito was well supplied with Marine stores so shopping for a new fiberglass dinghy was not a problem. The store where I found what I was looking for was about a quarter of a mile from where I was moored, so in the process of getting my new dingy to the boat, I got a good lesson in the art of rowing. This form of exercise would keep me in top physical shape for many years in the future. For one thing, rowing is extremely goal driven. When rowing ashore into a strong head wind, one does not stop for a rest lest the wind return you to where you began. Occasionally the need to continue rowing without a rest would test my endurance to the limit. Another interesting aspect of rowing is you are always facing the wrong way and can't see where you're going. I found if I would keep the point where I left in front of me; the place where I was headed would stay behind me. This makes sense only to anyone who has ever rowed a small boat.

Being in the middle of the "Hippie" era, Sausalito had its share of participants in that lifestyle. My social life at that time provided me with some unusual experiences. One evening at a party in a large houseboat, I accidentally got stoned on marijuana by just breathing the air. As my only drug of choice was alcohol, I had no idea what the affects of marijuana were. Later that night

I had set a course toward my boat's ghostly outline in the distance and believing I was nowhere close, unexpectedly rowed directly into its side. In my impaired condition, I should have rowed right past and missed it altogether.

Finally, my not having found a crew, Richard volunteered to try and make the trip to Hawaii with me. After loading all the supplies we would need, we sailed from Sausalito on our way at last and headed out under the Golden Gate Bridge. Richard had always suffered from motion sickness but he thought he could overcome it this time and was willing to give it a gallant try. Almost immediately after passing under the Golden Gate Bridge, he went below and lay down in the berth, never to reappear.

Not to be one to ever turn back, I decided to continue on seventy miles down the coast to the next good anchorage at Santa Cruz. This turned out to be yet one more of the smartest or the luckiest decision I could have made. Not having someone to relieve me, I was at the helm full time all the way to Santa Cruz. I was lucky to have a good following wind which made the trip comfortable for me but didn't do anything for Richard lying below. The large smooth swells created a regular undulation that only fed his discomfort.

We finally dropped anchor by the fisherman's pier off the boardwalk in Santa Cruz at nine in the evening. I had been at the helm nonstop for twelve hours without a break. I went below and after changing into dry clothes, made a supper of instant mashed potatoes and corn. Richard lay in a half comatose state looking at me. His only comment was, "You're incredible. Only an acidy cup of coffee this morning and then nothing all day and you can eat now."

With the boat gently rocking in the swell, I got a really good sleep that night.

The next morning, I rowed Richard ashore and he left, not to visit the boat again until years later.

Now here I was, still planning on sailing to Hawaii but I didn't want to try it without a crew.

Visiting back in Santa Clara a few days later, I was sitting in a company cafeteria with a group of girls I knew when one asked "What happened to your trip to Hawaii?" I explained how I had lost my crew and I was still looking for a replacement. Also I said this time I was trying to get a girl crew because they don't mind cooking, they bath regularly, and they are much more pleasant to look at than hairy legged old guys. I said I knew it would be difficult as not many are in the position of being able to just get up and leave their job and home on a moments notice.

To my surprise, I heard someone say, "I could do that." Incredibly, this comment came from a cute little blond sitting at the other end of the table. Answering to the name of Wendy Brown, she certainly got my attention. I asked if she was serious and when she assured me she was; I invited her out to the boat for a visit.

She drove down to Santa Cruz the next day and we spent a couple of hours on the boat talking. Before leaving she agreed to meet me on the Santa Cruz boardwalk on the following day.

As promised, she showed up and we walked up and down the boardwalk holding hands and talking for a long time. When she left, she said she was seriously thinking about going with me.

Now in case you have forgotten, this brings us up to the point where I backed up the story to Dallas.

So now on with the story

Are you ready?

Hurrah! Yippy! Just as the sun was setting, I saw Wendy walking out on the pier with a small duffel bag under one arm and a bottle of wine under the other. I knew this was very very good news. I kicked the old pelican that was living on the back of my dingy into the water and rowed over to the pier to get her.

Wendy needed a few weeks to settle all her affairs like giving notice at her work and selling her Volkswagen Bug. While she was getting things in order, she was staying part time in the apartment she shared with another girl and one night I tried staying with her. However leaving the boat unattended was too much for me and I drove back to the boat at 2 o'clock in the morning.

Getting ready to leave we spent a few pleasant weeks prowling the stores in Santa Cruz looking for provisions. The Fourth of July found us under the fire-works in Monterey harbor.

Later we hauled out on a sand bar at Moss Landing and repainted the boat bottom. We walked from the boat to the open air fruit and vegetable stand next to the harbor and did our daily shopping. A small plant nursery was located close by where we bought a potted eight inch high evergreen tree which added a bit of earth to our water world. That plant survived with us for many years.

It was summer and the weather in Monterey Bay was delightful. We were very fortunate to have had the good luck to be doing all these things and getting acquainted with each other without any sense of urgency about leaving.

# Chapter Three     Hawaii Bound

An uncountable number of days while building the boat I would sit on the levy by San Francisco Bay and watch the sun go down; imagining all the far off exotic places which were physically connected with the very water at my feet. I felt by touching this water, I was also touching them and now I was on my way to actually visiting these places instead of only dreaming about them.

The night before we left, anticipating many days at sea, Wendy and I treated ourselves to a final shore meal at the seafood restaurant on the Santa Cruz Boardwalk.

Finally late the next afternoon, with our dingy securely lashed on deck, we headed out of Monterey Bay and sailed west into the sunset. I thought at the time that this was absolutely as good as it can get but I was wrong. This was only the beginning of an unbelievable adventure.

Sorry but I have to break the mood and get a little technical at this point.

I had previously purchased a small book, Self Taught Navigation, to use for plotting our course to Hawaii. This book recommended using HO 249, a navigation method developed by the Air Force during WW2 for quickly arriving at a line of position while flying. I thought if it could be used while flying over two hundred miles an hour, I could use it sailing at no more than four miles an hour. So with a nautical almanac, HO 249 sight reduction tables, a fourteen dollar plastic sextant, and a ten dollar Timex quartz watch, we were on our way.

On our second day out, with land long out of sight, I decided to see how this celestial navigation thing worked. Some would think it foolhardy but I had not taken the opportunity to practice taking a line of sight in Monterey Bay before we left. I had read through the book several times and it didn't seem too complicated to me.

Now you are wondering, what's a line of sight?

Quite simply it is a line on a chart drawn ninety degrees to the direction of the sun. The location of this line is arrived at by first measuring the height of the sun with a sextant and then arriving at your location using the sight reduction tables. Sun sights taken in the morning, noon, and afternoon result in lines at different angles which cross at one point. This tells the observer where he is.

Or such is the claim.

After a week of sailing, we entered the warm tropical pacific waters and no longer needed clothing to keep warm. So we abandoned the practice altogether. Being nude creates an indescribable sense of freedom that cannot be achieved by any other means. Initially there is a feeling of being "Naked" which very soon fades and the loss of this naked feeling can be an embarrassment if it results in forgetting your condition in inappropriate places. The best quote I know in regard to this condition is "If God had wanted us to run around naked; we all would have been born that way."

Our days were filled with warm gentle winds and an unbroken deep blue world surrounded us. In a setting like this, how could anyone avoid falling in love. We were reveling in each other; often spontaneously making love where ever on the boat we happened to be. Lying completely open and unfettered in the sun is uniquely rewarding.

The boat was doing a masterful job of steering itself so we had no reason to be in the cockpit all the time. We would limit being on deck during the middle of the day because protection from the tropical sun was always needed to avoid a severe sunburn. After dark, we would often lie on the cockpit seat gazing up at the mast slowly drawing circles in the millions of stars that defined our ceiling. When the moon came up, it would only add to the already mystical feeling of being at sea at night. Lying there with music softly playing on our radio, there was something surreal about this little universe with everything needed for survival all alone in an unbroken expanse of darkness.

The days passed one after the other in a succession of unhurried calm. Occasionally we took turns reading out loud to each other from our collection of Paperback books and there was always the hypnotic rhythm of the waves to hold one's attention.

At after two weeks we had consumed all of our perishables and were reduced to eating only canned food. This wasn't a great sacrifice but it didn't help being daily reminded of better eating by "Aku Head", the Hilo radio station's morning Disc Jockey. This character would call Cafe 100 every morning to get a report on their current menu items. We could only fantasize about how good it will be when we arrive and can indulge ourselves in eating something other than canned fare.

We had on board a yummy supply of canned chicken, canned beef stew, canned tamales, canned chili, canned soup, canned three bean salad, canned Spam, canned sausage, canned baked beans, canned corn, canned peas, canned potatoes, and powered milk.

Get the point?

After twenty seven days at sea, the lines in my chart (which now resembled chicken tracks in the dust) indicated we should see Hawaii's tallest mountain sometime the next day.

Sure enough, around ten o'clock the next morning, I was sitting in the cockpit staring at the clouds on the distant horizon when I noticed one of them take on a strange dark conical shape. MOANA KEA!!!! This was the first proof I had that my navigation actually was working.

Later when asked what I would have done if I had been wrong and missed the Islands completely, I answered "I guess I would have had to continue west until I hit something. That is what Captain Cook did over two hundred years ago." There are hundreds of islands between Hawaii and Asia, the most notable being Japan.

Well here we were in Paradise.

We tied up at the State Pier in Hilo and checked in with the Harbor Master. Several large storage tanks next to the harbor permeated the air with the heavenly sweet odor of molasses and after breathing only sea air for almost a month, the feel and odor of the land was exhilarating.

I really like Hilo. It is the kind of place one should visit first after a long isolation at sea. It is a gentle reinsertion into the din of the populated world.

Down-town Hilo had the appearance of being lost in time.

Weather worn wooden two story building lined the main street and the only evidence of anything modern was a McDonald's. After sitting on the boat for so long with little real exercise, our legs were in much need of attention and we spent the better part of our days simply walking and exploring all the local sights.

Luckily for us the Hawaii State Fair opened shortly after we arrived and there, I had my first taste of Hawaiian food.

Wendy, having visited Hawaii previously, was familiar with most of the offerings and now acted as my native guide. I took an immediate and permanent liking to all of it. I was particularly partial to Kalua Pig and Poi. For those who have never been to Hawaii, Kalua Pig is moist shredded smoky flavored pork meat and Poi is a mashed slightly fermented starchy paste made from Taro roots.

After staying in this enchanting place for a week, we decided to move on.

Sailing north in the late afternoon along the Hamakua coast was uncomfortable with the strong trade winds constantly blowing a cold salty spray over us. It was well near midnight when we finally rounded Upolu point at the northern most part of the island and sailed down into the calm moon lit sea of the leeward coast. Here the warm flower laden odor of land filled the air and the only sound was the soft hiss of our hulls gliding smoothly through the serenely calm water. What a wonderful change from what we had been experiencing a short time earlier.

We sailed for the anchorage at Mahukona and were able to put in and drop the anchor there without mishap.

Now with the full moon over head and the boat gently rocking in the low swell, we lounged on deck and I let myself become part this time and place. I knew then I had found what I had been seeking for so long. This was a time and place of total and complete contentment.

The next morning we were off to the small boat anchorage at Kawaihae. This location enjoyed the convenience of a public park with showers, restrooms, and picnic tables. About a half a mile up the road, a small country store was the sole source of food in the area. Kawaihae is a large commercial harbor and between it and our anchorage, lay a large area of white coral debris excavated during the harbor's construction. This side of the island is quite hot and dry and one day while returning to the boat from the store, I was taking a shortcut across that hot white coral when I began feeling very distressed from the heat. Luckily I had purchased a frozen chicken and now, hopeing to ward off a heat stroke, I put it on my head under my hat.

Now I ask you, how many people do you know who would walk across a white coral beach with a frozen chicken under their hat? Don't laugh. Maybe it saved my life.

From here on to avoid sounding like a Travel Log, I will mention only things of interest and events occurring while we were at the many good anchorages around the islands.

#1 Kailua Kona.

A very touristy town. Here I bought my first pair of Hawaiian rubber slippers. While jumping to reach a fruit in a Papaya tree, I accidentally stepped on a ripe one on the ground and stained my brand new slippers. I don't seem to be able to keep anything, even for the shortest time, in a new condition.

#2 Kealakekua Bay.

This is the bay where Captain Cook, the discoverer of the Hawaiian Islands, first landed and was later killed in a dispute with the natives.

We decided to hike up an old Hawaiian foot path to the town of Captain Cook just above the bay. We were making good progress until about half the way up, the trail became overgrown with a tall sticky grass like plant which made continuing on impossible. But we were determined, so after returning to the head of the bay, we walked up the five mile long mountain road to town. Arriving very hot and tired, we bought a half gallon container of ice cream and sat down on the market steps and consumed it entirely on the spot. As we didn't have any form of refrigeration on the boat, we were always forced to quickly eat anything that could melt or spoil if left un-refrigerated.

#3 Kahena Beach, Maui.

Arriving late in the afternoon, we decided to rest and not go ashore until the next day. In the morning I discovered our dingy had become untied in the night and was missing. This was serious.

Except for the option of swimming, we were helplessly stranded on the boat. Panic finally yielded to simple apprehension and using my binoculars to scan, I began a search of the bay and shoreline. Much to my relief, I located our dingy half covered with sand upside down on the beach. Being responsible for its short try for freedom and having no other way to get to shore, I knew I would have to swim. We had gone swimming many times before at different anchorages and found the water in most places around the islands to be reasonably clear and clean but I was not prepared for the experience I would have swimming here. I dove in and while snorkeling toward the beach, I noticed the water at about the thirty foot depth became so clear and the bottom so visible it created the allusion that I was floating high in the air instead of in the water. Always having suffered from acrophobia, I started to panic; afraid I might fall to the bottom. This was totally irrational but my fear was real never the less. With steely nerves I continued on and without falling to the bottom, gratefully made it to the beach. Finding the oars still stowed under the seat was a big relief and I was able to row back to the boat. This was a lesson in being more diligent in securing the dingy. I was very lucky this time.

#4 Mala Wharf, Maui.

In need of fresh water, we went ashore here to see what was available. The first possibility we spotted was a church with a "Jesus Coming Soon" sign on their roof. Here in the good tradition of Christians, they refused us water saying if they gave us some, they would have to give water to everyone who came by. Now wouldn't that be an unacceptable sacrifice.

A little way further down the street we came to a Buddhist Temple and they, Buddha blessum, gladly let us fill our jugs.

#5 Lahaina, Maui. The next day was Nov. 25, Thanksgiving day. Wendy and I debated what we should have for dinner and we again decided on ice cream. This may seem strange but anything cold was a great treat and as we were trying to make our funds last as long as possible, eating at any of the Restaurants would be much more expensive. Our Thanksgiving Dinner was therefore a half gallon of pumpkin ice-cream consumed while sitting under Lahaina's famous Banyan tree.

Skip the next paragraph if you, like me, couldn't care less about the history of this stupid tree we were sitting under. But if you must, read on.

The original tree was brought here from India and was only eight feet high when planted in 1873. The unique way a Banyan tree grows is to periodically put down feelers from its extended limbs and when this feeler makes contact with the ground it sprouts roots and becomes a new trunk. This new trunk now puts out its own limbs and the process is repeated over and over. The result is this tree currently stands over sixty feet high, has twelve major trunks in addition to its massive core and covers an area equal to five house lots.

#6 Kahalui, Maui.

The harbor here has a population of fish I found nowhere else in Hawaii. Schools of fish called Half-beaks call this Harbor home. Their name was derived from their lower jaw extending far out in front like a sword fish. These fish are related to flying fish and have a similar reaction to being disturbed. Our first encounter with them occurred one night while we were returning to our boat in the dingy. I was rowing along in the dark when suddenly I felt a commotion between my feet. Looking with my flashlight, I was amazed to see several shinny small fish flopping about. It seems, when frightened, these fish jump frantically out of the water to escape their perceived predators and in so doing, would accidentally land in our dingy. These were very delicate white meat fish and we enjoyed them at breakfast sautéed with sliced almonds in a little butter. Thereafter whenever we felt like having fish for dinner, I would simply row around until enough fish had obligingly jumped into my dingy.

One day Wendy and I rode our bicycles up the steep two mile long road from the Harbor to the picturesque old town of Wailuku. From here down to Maalaea on the southern coast of the island, was an almost continuous seven mile long down hill road which we found too tempting to resist. Being able to coast a bicycle for seven miles is a rare treat. Fortunately another inland road on the flat was available for the return trip to Kahalui.

Hold it! You are probably wondering where these bicycles came from. Well I forgot to mention we had bought two small folding bicycles when we were in Lahaina. Sorry about that. It's probably not any more interesting now than it would have been back then but it does give you a break in this breathtaking narrative.

Kahalui had a small shopping center where we were lucky to be present when a Hawaiian Concert was happening. The well known Hawaiian group, The Makaha Sons of Niihau, was featured as well as lesser known performers and we spent a very pleasant couple of hours sitting in the shade listing to their music. It was the small unexpected things like this that made living like we were so special.

Leaving Kahalui, we planned to anchor off the beach on the west coast of Molokai but darkness had fallen by the time we arrived so we decided to continue on across the Molokai channel and anchor in the Ala Wai Yacht Harbor on Oahu.

This channel, like the Alenuihaha, can be quite rough and it was that night. The bright lights of Oahu's east coast appeared as a sparkling jeweled apparition in the distance and then just as quickly disappeared as the boat lifted and dropped on the large surging waves we were now riding. In the bottom between the swells, the blackness was complete. This only amplified the hissing sound of the breaking wave crests building behind us. After four hours of this roller coaster ride, it was a welcome relief to be rounding Diamond Head and sailing into the calm waters off Waikiki Beach. The millions of lights along this strip of the coast made recognizing any landmarks quite difficult.

Luckily I spotted the sea buoy off the Harbor and turned in there. My published sailing instructions indicated an anchorage could be had in its turning basin but after entering, I discovered this was no longer true. The channel here had no depth markers and as a result, while trying to leave, we ran aground next to the sea wall. It was now two o'clock in the morning and I was getting a little tired but I couldn't stay where I was.

I dropped an anchor out from the boat to use as an attachment and while pulling on the rope, the boat suddenly broke free, throwing me off balance into the water. This was getting to be a little too much variety for me.

I had no choice but to continue on a few miles further down

the coast to the next likely anchorage at Keehi Lagoon. This is a large well protected former seaplane landing sight with the State Small Boat Harbor on its eastern edge and Honolulu international Airport opposite on the west. Its large barrier reef and excellent holding ground made this anchorage the most popular spot on the island.

After sailing uneventfully up the long narrow channel entrance, we dropped anchor just inside the lagoon. It had been a long stressful night so with great relief, we collapsed in our bed and immediately fell asleep.

Three hours later at six o'clock, our peaceful rest abruptly ended when a 747 Jumbo Jet flew in our front hatch and out the back. Or so it seemed. We had anchored directly under the end of the airport runway and the aircraft taking off had gained only a few hundred feet as it passed over us. This was not a good spot for a long term visit.

Moving our boat further into the lagoon, we found a much better anchorage across the channel from a coral beach. This beach also provided a convenient place to leave our dingy when we went ashore. After getting directions from a local, we walked the ten blocks to the closest grocery store. While walking back, Wendy broke her rubber slipper and was forced to walk with one bare foot for part of the way. When this became too uncomfortable for her, I got a chance to be a hero and wrapped my tee-shirt around her foot to fashion a sort of slipper which provided some protection from the hot road. This was all a part of living the good life.

Keehi Lagoon was a safe place to stay but because of its commercial use and closeness to the airport, it could hardly be thought of as paradise. Consequently we decided to look for an anchorage somewhere more exotic.

After studying the map of Oahu, we decided Pokai Bay on the west coast looked the most promising. This bay, located next to the town of Waianae, was well protected from the ocean swells by a long breakwater and was equipped with a small boat loading dock where fresh water was available. The park next to the bay also provided cold water showers and rest rooms for swimmers and picnickers. Being on the lee side of the island, this area enjoys fair weather most of the year. These were ideal conditions for an extended visit. We had an unobstructed view of sunsets on the water and the frequent showers in the mountains behind us created beautiful double rainbows many afternoons.

Please forgive me for waxing ecstatic about this place but it deserves all the praise I can give it.

We settled in and took each day as it came. We were in easy walking distance to all the stores in town and with our mail delivered to General Delivery at the Post Office, we had found a home. Wendy began taking Hula lessons and through the people she met, she became immersed in the Hawaiian culture.

We took advantage of the twenty five cent, unlimited distance, bus fare available and often visited Honolulu and Waikiki Beach. The main bus terminal at the Ala Moana Shopping Center was the hub for all the different bus routes and from there, for the same twenty five cents, we could ride completely around the island.

I apologize if this is starting to sound a little dull but sometimes only ordinary things happen in life. I suppose you could argue that living on an unlimited vacation with a beautiful girl on a boat in Hawaii is not ordinary but by now it had become so to me. Don't get me wrong. Not a single day passed without my being aware of my good fortune.

Enough of this psychological drivel and on with the story.

Our stay in Pokai Bay was interrupted only when we sailed to Hanalei Bay on Kauai for a short visit. On our way, after darkness had fallen, we were witness to a once in a lifetime phenomenon. The moon behind us was shining through a light rain shower which created a light gray misty "rainbow" which persisted for quite a few minutes before slowly fading away. The magic of that sight lingered long after.

It was full daylight when we arrived at Hanalei and after finding a convenient place to anchor; we lay below and had a short nap. Later in the afternoon while lounging topside, we observed a young couple rowing toward us. The friendly expectant looks on their faces told me they planned to stop and say hello. Not feeling up to greeting visitors, I told Wendy, "Pretend we're not at home."

The uniqueness of my boat design had attracted their attention and as it frequently happened they wanted to have a look. I had to live with the inevitable result of having a boat that looks very different. It turned out; the visiting couple had just arrived, having sailed straight to Hanalei Bay from San Francisco. They told us they sail over every year and had planed to return to California without stopping at any of the other islands in Hawaii. This seemed a little strange to me but I think everyone should sail his own course.

One afternoon we accidentally discovered a fun diversion. We were brushing into the water, a few scraps of cabbage which had fallen on the deck while we were making our dinner and I noticed there seemed to be a lot of turbulence in the water around these bits of green. On closer inspection we discovered this was caused by many small puffer fish arguing over this unexpected food source. These fish of course are inedible but we couldn't resist trying to catch them anyway. So with a bit of our salad tied to a string, we set about tempting them. Now the fun began. A fish would make a grab at the bait and when we gently pulled on the string, they would hang on until they were about a foot out of the water. Probably thinking this wasn't such a good idea after all; they would eventually release their hold and drop back into the water. I guess this was a childish game but like many others, these were the ones fondly long remembered.

The Hanalei River enters the bay here and can be navigated upstream in small boats. Wendy and I rowed our dingy up this river, past flooded taro fields and wetland forest, to a popular waterside restaurant. This place was more easily reached by car on the road but we enjoyed the adventure of doing things the hard way and besides, we had no car. The exercise just made our steak dinner all the more satisfying. On a bluff inland from the bay is a Club Med resort and we sometimes would feel superior living and enjoying all this without having to pay for it.

Damn it, here I go writing for the travel guides again. Well bare with me and we'll soon get to better stuff.

After a pleasant week in Hanalei we sailed on around the island to the main port of Nawilliwilli.

The small boat harbor there was being used as a set for

filming the movie, Acapulco Gold. My boat, quite accidentally, was included in the background of three scenes early in the story. This Nawilliwilli location was represented in the movie as being in Mexico. We sat on deck and watched them setting up their shots for a while and finally came to the conclusion that watching the filming of a movie is near the top of the list of lives most boring activities.

Years later when I had the good fortune to get a copy of this movie, I found I was thoroughly entertained by it. If a movie is bad enough it becomes a lot of fun to watch and that was what, for me, saved this one.

Back in Pokai Bay I started playing around with the idea of making a major change to the boat. The center hull was only twenty feet long and I decided I would like to replace it with one thirty six feet in length. This would allow me to increase the mast height and sail area resulting in greater speed and hopefully, a better, smoother ride.

Luckily I knew a local character named Phil Kelly who had introduced himself on the very first day we arrived in Pokai Bay. Phil was strange man consumed by terminal generosity who was always inviting us out on his old wooden boat for a night of fishing. I enjoyed these trips as there was always a lot more fishing than there was catching. A spotlight on the water was supposed to attract the fish but this never seemed to work. All I ever saw were swarms of tiny insect size creatures swirling around in the water. However it was a pleasant way to spend a few hours on a warm summer evening.

He also was some sort of a born again believer who didn't trust Doctors and as a result, all his children were born at home with only his assistance. His wife, Cora, was a sweet, patient soul who tolerated Phil's propensity for turning their living room into a workshop while repairing his boat related gear.

His help was a great assistance to me in my new project. I had talked about my plans for modifying my boat with him and one day he introduced me to Bob Stienky, another entry on Phil's endless list of friends. Talking with Bob, I found he owned a property in the country with a large covered shed behind his house and after I explained what my plans for the boat were, he agreed to rent his shed to me for forty dollars a month.

In keeping with our healthy athletic life style, every day while building the new hull, Wendy and I would commute the three miles to Bob's house on our bicycles. The road into the country was for the most part flat but it did have at one place, a long very slight incline which we called Killer Hill. When going back to the boat after a days work, Killer Hill was now a welcome down hill assist. Part of the varied atmosphere here in the country was the hog farm located just to the windward of our location. Every morning they would cook up a batch of feed for the pigs and its pungent odor would drift over us. This was a little much but I suppose some sacrifices have to be made if one wants to achieve ones goals.

Let me rewrite that lofty tolerant last sentence.

Every morning they would cook up a batch of feed for the pigs and its stinking odor was so thick, if it hadn't been for the flies in the way, you could have seen it.

I can not over emphasize Wendy's good hearted support and the help she gave to me during this time. If she had thought in the beginning this was all going to be relaxing on the foredeck with martinis in the afternoon, she was soon disillusioned. She never once complained or expressed any dissatisfaction with the way things were going. She was a real trooper and I was very fortunate to have found her.

The next item I needed was finding a place where I could haul the boat out of the water and exchange the small hull for the new larger one. I had earlier noticed a vacant lot behind the post office which looked like a good choice. Only a few hundred yards from the boat launching ramp in Pokai Bay with no obstacles in the way, it presented a perfect solution to my problem. I contacted the owner of this lot by phone and asked if I could rent it for awhile to do some boat work. The person I was talking with seemed hesitant; saying there was a family involved and asked me how long I would need it. I answered; I thought no more than a couple of weeks. After a moment he told me to just go ahead and use it, only don't make a mess. I didn't make a mess but I was a little off on my time estimate. My two week estimate stretched into seven months and thankfully, no one said a word.

For electricity, I strung an extension chord to the house of an elderly couple across the street and agreed to pay part of their electric bill for the privilege. As the result of this association, I was also obliged to convert their food stamps into dollars so the old man could buy cigarettes and beer. This was a strange couple who frequently had a falling out resulting in the wife sitting in their car for various lengths of time until she was allowed back in the house. Thinking back now, I wonder why this sort of thing seemed to be nobody's business but theirs'. There was never any physical abuse that I was aware of so I guess a little time out was tolerated or maybe she just got tired of hearing his voice.

Next door to their house was a county sponsored hostel which regularly housed a variety of characters. One unfortunate lady who lived there, for some reason always had her head partially shaved and she would occasionally leave food like pizza or bottles of Pepsi under my boat. For some reason, she never stopped or tried to talk to us. Another resident here, I believe was a war vet. He lived entirely in his own world and was forever walking up and down the streets of the town; occasionally breaking into violent arguments with an imagined companion who always seemed to accompany him.

It was during this time I had the good fortune to meet Jean-Louis Lependu and his lovely Tahitian wife, Lovina. Jean-Louis was an Officer in the Merchant Marine and we soon found we had much in common. Lovina was active in the local Hula Dancing Club and Wendy eagerly joined her in that pastime. Living close by in Waianae, they welcomed us into their home and many evenings were spent over a few beers and sea stories. Inevitably over the years they were destined to become my lifelong friends.

Well back to rebuilding the boat.

This project presented a once in a lifetime picture when removing the center hull left a gaping hole running down the middle bottom of the boat. As we were living in it the entire time, we needed a floor to walk on. So I parked Phil's old yellow pickup truck underneath and by walking in the truck bed we could use the galley and get into the births. I suppose it looked strange when all you could see between the boat bottom and the truck bed were our legs walking back and forth.

This rebuilding of the boat turned into a much larger job than I had anticipated and I ended up doing much more than just replacing the center hull. I completely rebuilt the cockpit and laminated the decks with a non-skid material.

Another spooky good luck thing happened at this time. My original center hull had molded in water tanks and I initially planned to do the same with the new ones. Rethinking the idea, I thought it would be much better if I were to install removable plastic containers instead. Finding four fifteen gallon plastic barrels which were perfect for the job, I couldn't believe my luck to find they fit perfectly under the cabin floor. It was as though I had measured them first. A sixteenth of an inch bigger and they wouldn't have worked.

Finally at last I was finished and after successfully launching the boat, I decided to sail back to Keehi where there were better facilities for changing the mast and re-rigging.

Thinking back now I marvel at my blind optimism regarding the use of that location in Waianae as long as I needed it and not told to leave post haste by the owners or even the police if there was some sort of zoning restriction. Maybe this was one of those times when it is easier to get forgiveness than to get permission.

Back in Keehi, I began working on a couple different ideas I had in regard to the new sail plan I wanted. The need of a facility with large sewing capacity put me in contact with a character self named "Omar the Tent Man". Omar was a big friendly Swede who owned a tent and awning manufacturing and rental business. This exactly fit my need and his establishment became a second home. He ran his business in a rather strange way, meaning his philosophy was "last in, first out." If a job got buried under a later arrival, there was a good chance it would end up further and further down and never emerge. I of course didn't know this at first so when after a couple days waiting for my job to emerge, I complained a bit. His response was "Do you know how to run a sewing machine?" When I answered somewhat unsure that I believed I could master it, he replied, "Here's a key. Be sure to lock up when you leave." From that day on until he sold out ten years later, I had unlimited access to the place.

Years later when I informed him I thought one of his trusted employs was stealing from him, his reply was "Well, they aren't taking it all."

It was now on Wendy's insistence that I went to the Tuberculin Clinic in Honolulu to check up on my lung condition.

Lung condition???

Didn't I tell you about that?

Well back in California while I was still building the boat, all activity came to a temporary halt when I decided to have a physical checkup. I had developed an annoying intermittent bussing in my head which I wanted to check out. I had not had an occasion to see a Doctor since leaving the Navy twelve years earlier and I should have known better than to give a doctor a chance to find something wrong. It has been my experience that given the chance, they always will.

I was told a spot on my left lung showed up on my x-rays. All the tests they gave me to ascertain the cause of my affliction came back negative. Lacking any evidence to the contrary, my doctor made the assumption that it was lung cancer. I was only thirty seven years old at the time and had been smoking over twenty years which added to the likelihood he was right.

I was immediately checked into the Hospital for a needle biopsy of lung tissue and a lymph node removal.

Without leaving the Hospital, I was scheduled for lung removal two days later. On the morning of the planned surgery, I was given my happy shot and wheeled down to the operating room. While I was waiting my turn just outside the operating room doors, my doctor made a final call to pathology to see if a culture had been grown from my biopsy.

Good News! I didn't have cancer. What I did have was a Atypical Acid-fast Bacterial Infection. That meant I had a strange form of Tuberculosis.

Thinking back at my lack of concern at the time is a little frightening. At the time I would have let them remove one of my lungs without a second opinion.

Originally the prescribed treatment in California was a regiment of shots every other day for an indefinite length of time but after a month or so I got tired of the whole thing and just stopped getting them.

Now picking up the story where I left off in Hawaii, I went to the TB clinic and after bringing them up to date; they immediately wanted me in isolation. That meant no close contact with people. This of course meant I wouldn't be able to have a job and expose the public to my affliction.

Ah Ha! This restriction automatically made me eligible for welfare. This was a lucky stroke as we had almost exhausted our monetary reserves while rebuilding the boat.

They put me on a drug routine consisting of every drug known to have any affect on TB. This meant I was taking thirteen pills a day. This isn't all bad news because I was very lucky to be living in Hawaii.

Do to the high incident of TB in the immigrant population; the state financed all treatment to assure no one would go untreated for financial reasons. They said I could go to work as soon as my monthly sputum test turned negative and there was a two year requirement of negative results before medication could stop.

My test went negative after only one month so I now was off welfare. I was required to register with the state employment agency and look for a job. Here is where it gets spooky. In order to not rush into this work thing, I thought if I declared my occupation as Printed Circuit Designer, I would be perfectly safe from landing a job and I could stay on welfare. In a state where conveyer belts in the pineapple cannery were considered state of the art engineering, this should have been easy to do.

BEEEEEP!!!! WRONG!!

Tom Moore, a local telephone company equipment sales representative had just started a company called Intelect. His plan was to start building, instead of buying, the equipment he was selling. As a favor to a friend in the State Employment Office, he had listed a requirement for a Printed Circuit Designer. At my subsequent interview with Tom, I was unable to talk him out of hiring me and as a result, I had the only Printed Circuit Design job in the entire state. Luckily this job with Intelect was at first only part time. I bought a motorcycle and, as Wendy had gotten a job at a hotdog and ice-cream concession on Waikiki Beach and we were, regrettably, back in the rat race.

However "Rat Race" Hawaiian style still has it all over any other version.

A few months after starting the part time job at Intelect, I had an opportunity to go into a full time position at the University of Hawaii's Institute of Astronomy. I told Tom if he could pay me one hundred dollars a month, I wouldn't take the University job. He was hesitant about committing to anything so I accepted the University's offer. We were designing and building the computer control for the infrared telescope being installed on top of Mouna Kea on the Big Island.

The location of our office at the University was up a deep valley in the mountains opposite Waikiki where the normal weather most of the year has the trade winds blowing the ever-present rain sideways rather than downward. Regardless of how nice the weather was on the boat in the morning, I would always take my rain gear with me when I headed for work. I would frequently ride down to Waikiki and have lunch with Wendy and I always carried my rain gear with me. On a day with strong trade winds blowing, it was not unusual to get rained on in Waikiki while the sun was shining brightly overhead. I remember thinking one day there was something strange about this. Analyzing my thoughts, I realized what was strange was I didn't think it was strange that it was raining while the sun was shining.

Don't spend too much time on that last sentence.

There I go again with the Travel Log thing again. It's a slippery slope that's hard to avoid..

OK, just one more short paragraph about this job and I'll shut up about it.

At the completion of the design phase at the University, I had to help install the equipment in the telescope building on top of the mountain on the Big Island. This meant working on Mouna Kea at thirteen thousand feet above sea level. I soon realized I was a sea level creature. Even in Base Camp at nine thousand feet, I was not a happy camper. Fortunately my part of the job there on the mountain was not extensive and after two weeks I was back on my boat where I belonged.

Finally after my TB treatments were over, we were ready to resume our too long delayed extended trip south. We quit or jobs and left Keehi Lagoon on our way into the South Pacific.

Hold it.

Not so fast.

First we had to stop in Pokai bay and say goodbye to all our friends there. Then there was an opportunity to anchor for a while in Waimea Bay. Another extended delay occurred between the popular Sand Bar in the middle of Kaneohe Bay and additionally the good anchorage by the YWCA. While at the Sand Bar, we were anchored next to a young man who commuted on a Windsurfer from his boat to his job on Coconut Island. He could step off his boat onto that board and take off with no more apparent effort than someone stepping on an escalator. Coming back to the boat in the evening, he would sail up and step off the board and onto his deck with the same aplomb he exhibited when he left. That took some practice.

The only thing I disliked about Kaneohe Bay was its location on the Eastern side of the mountains. I am never awake in time to see or appreciate a sunrise but I do enjoy sunsets. There were never any sunsets here. About three o'clock in the afternoon, the sun would just go out as it disappeared into the ever present gray clouds on the mountain tops. The rest of the day would be a depressing gloom.

Retracing the original course we sailed when we arrived three years before, we were off on our way to Molokai. After a short stop at an abandoned little landing which had formally been used to load cattle, we headed for the pineapple port of Kaumalapau on Lanai. After one more stop at Lahaina, Kahalui, and Hana on Maui, it was across the Alinuihaha Channel to Kawaihae. Retracing our original path down the Big Island coast brought us finally to Okoi Bay. This was the last anchorage available before entering the broad Pacific. After taking a deep breath here, we were finally headed south.

# Chapter Four    Sailing South

It had taken us seven months just to get out of Hawaii.

You probably have noticed I have lost my biting humor and have lapsed into a state of sentimental nostalgic reminiscences. I can't help it because these times were so special compared with the earlier parts of my life. From here on I will try not to get too bogged down in trivia and keep it light and interesting.

Fanning Island, laying seven hundred miles to the south, was our first goal. We had good steady winds and a week later my late afternoon sun-sight put us only about forty five miles north of the island.

As Fanning was small and lightly populated, I could not depend on any shore lights to guide us and not wanting to come onto it in the dark, I decided to shorten sail and just ghost along during the night. At daylight the next morning, even though no island was visible, I continued on course toward where I thought it lay. I was unable to get a sun-sight as the sky was overcast all that day. Late afternoon still didn't reveal an island so I thought we had sailed past it somehow. Using the philosophy of when in doubt, do nothing, I decided to heave to for the night and wait for the next day. Luckily in the morning the sky was clear and after I got my first line of position, I couldn't believe the results. I waited an hour and took another sight which confirmed my first one. Not only had we not passed the Island but were now fifty miles further away than we had been thirty-six hours earlier. Something was very wrong. I trusted my navigation so I dug out all the charts I had on this part of the ocean and AHA! There it was. The ocean in this area had a sixty mile a day eddy current which had flipped us back north while we were hove to and ghosting along.

Skip the next paragraph if you want to avoid a geographic lesson.

Fanning is not really an island but an Atoll. These are formed when an island surrounded by reefs sinks leaving a central shallow lagoon surrounded by small narrow palm covered coral islets. The lagoon is usually filled and emptied by the tidal flow through an opening in the reef called the Pass. This tidal current can be very swift and can make entering or leaving the lagoon difficult. The best time for traversing is either with the current or during the slack time between the flows.

End of geographic lesson.

Approaching the Island near sundown and not wanting to try the pass without knowing the state of the tide, we anchored outside the reef and were treated to the most brilliant sundown I have ever seen.

Luckily, the water was slack in the morning and we safely entered and anchored just inside the lagoon next to a collection of tin roofed copra sheds. After checking in with the local authorities, we set out to explore the island. The people here were all very friendly and gave us what assistance they could. They were all temporary workers, imported with their families to harvest copra (coconut) and as a result of the temporary nature of their existence; their living accommodations were pretty basic. Their housing consisted of corrugated tin huts and they made small gardens by filling in low depressions in the coral with whatever soil was available. Here they raised a meager crop of taro, banana, and cassava.

We were told there was a small store that was unpredictably open for one hour each day and a bell would ring signaling its availability. Responding to the sound of the bell later in the afternoon, we found the so called store was only a small shed exhibiting for sale, a sack of flour, a sack of onions, a sack of sugar, some fish-hooks, and one transistor radio. They told us we were lucky to have onions as they did not last long in the tropical heat. We were able to resist spending too much money here. I did replenish my gasoline supply delivered in a stained plastic bucket filled from a rusty fifty-five gallon drum.

There were only two sources of fresh water on the island. One was rain runoff from the copra sheds' tin roofs and the other from shallow wells dug in the coral. The first had a slight rust color and had a high mineral component from the natural aerial deposits emanating from the hundreds of Frigate birds circulating overhead. This water was also populated by small wiggly things which required screening out before using. The well water was clear but tasted brackish from seawater seepage. I had four independent water tanks on the boat and as we had almost emptied one, I decided to fill it with the shed runoff and use this water only for washing dishes and bathing.

The people here have a strange unique way of greeting a passerby. When we pass someone coming our way we say Hello or Hi, whereas in a similar situation, they would simply say "Good By." Maybe it is an English version of the native language custom of one person leaving saying "I am leaving" and the one remaining saying "I am staying".

A couple days after our arrival we were joined by another small yacht. The friendly couple on board had spent a year in Tahiti and they were now on their way north to Hawaii. We spent an enjoyable evening swapping sea stories and comparing notes on Hawaii. They were eager to be on their way and while leaving the next day they somehow left one of their anchors on the bottom. I notified one of the local families of the anchors location and was rewarded with a large parrot fish which we immediately cooked in our small charcoal oven. Parrot fish are fine eating.

This is how we found this Island in 1980 and I can only guess what has happened as the result of it later becoming a stopover on a Hawaiian Cruise Line itinerary. Foreign registry ships cannot call at US Ports without touching a foreign port once on each cruise so to get around that restriction, the cruise line uses tiny Fanning Island as a foreign port while basically only cruising the Hawaii Islands.

I can never get too much of island life but the diversions here were really limited and after three days of rest we bid farewell to this remote place.

On our way again, I was below resting one night with the boat sailing itself when a sudden squall blew up. I went up on deck in total darkness with the intention of putting up a smaller sail. Just as I removed the shackle pin on the bottom of the sail, a sudden gust jerked the sail and knocked the pin out of my hand and it disappeared into the blackness. I was in a real fix now because I could not release my grip on the sail and go below to get another pin as the sail, being unsecured, would have violently flailed around and possibly damaged the rigging. I was kneeling next to a small spray shield by the forward hatch and not having any other choice, I reacted to impulse and ran my hand along its length and there, Hurray! I found my errant shackle pin. If that pin had landed an inch further out on the other side, it would have rolled off the deck and been lost forever. After replacing the shackle, I thought I better stop fixing things and returned to the calm of my cabin; leaving the boat to thereafter take care of its self.

Another week of uneventful sailing brought us to Pago Pago Bay in American Samoa. We entered and turned up the dogleg toward the head of the bay when I noticed we were being blown sideways toward the fish cannery on the bay's lee shore and I could do nothing to bring the bow around. I had forgotten we had been sailing down wind and the Dagger Board was raised. I fortunately remembered just in time and called to Wendy to kick it down. That worked and a little shaken but back in control, I continued on up the Bay and tied up with a group of other yachts in Pago Pago Harbor. ( the Appendix will explain how and why this worked)

As American Samoa is an unincorporated territory of the United States, I assumed as a citizen, I wouldn't have a problem here. I was wrong. After tying up, I went ashore and did some shopping for fresh bread and eggs. When I returned to the boat, I was greeted by their immigration and customs officials who were somewhat upset that I had failed to check in with them first. And besides, now it was after normal working hours and they were on overtime. It took a little persuading and a bit of bribing to pacify them but we were finally cleared.

Later, swapping sea stories with our neighbors on the boat next to us, we learned we had been out sailing in the hurricane season.

Hurricane Season???? Somehow I had missed that fact. Our new friends highly recommended that we stay here in Samoa until the end of the hurricane season in April. With about a dozen other yachts to visit and water and electricity available, it wasn't a bad place to spend some time. Wendy as usual made friends with some of the local families and got into their culture, weaving mats and hats. One negative here, the small boat harbor was directly across the bay from the tuna fish cannery and when the wind came from that direction, the atmosphere became quite "fishy." Fortunately this didn't happen often.

One unpleasant condition during this season was the humidity and temperature both hovered above ninety most of the time. It was nearly impossible to dry anything. There was one advantage though. If you happened to get caught in the rain, it was a welcome relief from the heat and besides, you couldn't get any wetter. Our small electric fan was the only thing which made it possible to sleep at night.

Also the limited variety of food available here was very irritating. There were American style stores with a lot of canned goods but they were short on fresh meat and vegetables. One common offering in all of them was frozen chicken backs. No legs, breasts, or wings. Only backs???

The only redeeming item here was Violima, the local beer named after Robert Louis Steven's home in Western Samoa.

Pago Pago had a small movie theater which was not much more than a large room with wooden chairs for seating. The only time I attended, the movie was a Peter Sellers comedy and at first I thought it was some sort of "arty" film as everything had a hazy, foggy look. I was wrong. This effect was created by a totally inadequate light source in the projector. The lack of illumination was compensated for by the ear splitting sound system. I sat through the entire movie protecting my hearing from permanent damaged by keeping my fingers pressed firmly in my ears.

Transportation here on the island was provided by small garishly painted busses built on compact car frames. Wooden bench seats and Plexiglas windows, if any existed at all defined the interior. Also included next to the driver was an obligatory speaker playing very loud Samoan Music. One advantage though, was the total lack of bus stops. Entry and exit could be had anywhere on the road. A strange custom practiced by the Samoans was the construction of a burial tomb in the middle of the yard directly in the front of their houses. Another was their enthusiasm for the English game of Cricket. This game was frequently played in the rain and mud and was always accompanied by their fans incessantly drumming on empty biscuit tins.

After five months the hurricane season was over and it was safe to go sailing again so we headed for the Islands of Western Samoa. This was only a short sail of about a hundred miles.

We found checking in here at Apia to be a much more pleasant experience than we had in American Samoa.

I thoroughly enjoyed poking around their native market and trying all the local foods. Many of the small concessions offered hot plates of different meats and vegetables. I even tried lamb flaps and baked bananas, a dish which was and will remain totally foreign to me. My all time favorite though, was an egg sized ball of flour and banana dough, deep fried in beef fat. This artery blocking delight with the unlikely name of "Panee Cakee" turned out to be my undoing. I couldn't eat just one. A half a dozen would disappear down my throat before I knew what happened.

Many of the Polynesian renditions of English words sound strange because no words in their language end with a consonant. So having no practice forming that sound, they simply add vowels where necessary. Pan Cake becomes Panee Cakee.

The Samoans somehow had gotten hooked on beef fat by the early explorers of these islands and now it was imported from Australia in five gallon tins. Another important import in similar tins was corned beef. It seems the local name for corned beef originated when an English cook on a ship was making pea soup with corned beef as an additive. Misunderstanding a local's question about what he was preparing, he answered "Pea Soup." From that time on, corned beef would be known as Pea Souppo.

Panee Cakee and Cocoa Samoa made from locally grown cocoa beans made up a significant part of our diet at the time.

The only unpleasant part of our stay happened while we were anchored in a small inlet next to the market. Our anchor chain became fouled with all the refuse dumped into the water there. A floating mass of trimmings from all the produce cleaned at the market was mixed with the unexplainable addition of animal matter like dead rats and even once a small dead pig. Having to clear our anchor chain from this tangled mass was not something one bragged about in a travel brochure.

One tourist attraction here in Apia is certainly worth expending a little energy to see. This would be Robert Louis Steven's Burial Site. Situated on the top of a high hill behind the town, it can be visited by walking up a long winding trail through the undergrowth. This was a little tiring but well worth the effort. I found the side of his tomb inscribed with these words.

> *Under the wide and starry sky.*
> *Dig the grave and let me lie.*
> *Glad did I live and gladly die.*
> *And I laid me down with a will.*
> *This be the verse you grave for me.*
> *Here he lies where he longed to be.*
> *Home is the sailor, home from the sea.*
> *And the hunter home from the hill.*

I have never read a more moving epitaph.

I can see how one could form a strong sentimental attachment to these beautiful islands.

Wendy and I of course had to stop in for a drink and catch the Polynesian show at Aggie Grays. We were also treated to a cold raw fish and coconut dish which I liked very much. This was at the time the most famous hotel in this part of the world and come to think of it, at the time, the only famous hotel in this part of the world.

Finally needing to keep on with our cruise south we next stopped at Western Samoa's largest island, Savaii. We anchored in a large protected bay where every day a small fleet of sail driven fishing boats would skim back and forth past us in the gray morning light. They would all disappear at full sunrise as I suppose the fish were no longer available then.

One morning a local man rowed his canoe out to our boat and using a rudimentary form of pigeon-english asked if we liked palasomi (a dish made from taro leaves and coconut milk) and taro. I indicated we do eat those things and he, smiling, left only to return a little later with a basket full of these afore mentioned items. Climbing onto our boat he indicated he wanted to have lunch with us and did we have any canned fish to contribute to the menu. After he selected sardines from our assortment of canned sardines, tuna, salmon, and mackerel, we sat down to eat. Due to the lack of a common language, not much was said but I could tell he really liked the sardines. The proof of this was born out when, after all the fish were consumed, he drank with relish all the oil that the fish had been packed in. This was a man who probably had fresh fish every day of his life but who considered this canned variety a great treat.

Here on Savaii we met a New Zealand expatriate who was working for the Samoan government maintaining a mountain top radio facility. I have never had a more un-nerving ride in my life than the one he gave us. We rode with him in his four wheel drive jeep up through the trackless rain forest to the top of that mountain. He apparently knew the correct way to go but many times I could not identify anything that looked like a trail let alone a road. The wheels would frequently bog down in the soft rain soaked earth but after a few tries, we would manage to lurch forward again. I tried to note our position as we went; thinking if I was the only one to survive the inevitable destruction of the jeep, I could find my way back down the mountain. Obviously we made it safely or I wouldn't be here writing this. That was a real memorable trip.

There was another distinctive feature on this bay that I saw nowhere else in my travels. All the outhouses here were built out in the water ten or twenty feet away from the shore and connected to the land with a wooden walkway. This method of sanitation simplified the problem of flushing the toilet but I would imagine swimming was discouraged.

After a pleasant week here, it was time to move on. The next Island on our map was Iles De Wallis or in English, Wallis Island. This island was a French territory and I would come to appreciate here, the great difference in the way various governments conduct their business. I recalled in American Samoans I was asked "When are you leaving." Here I was asked "How long are you staying."

But I'm getting ahead of myself. As we approached Wallis Island in the late afternoon, a small power boat approached and gestured for us to follow them through the only pass in the reef that was safe to use. As soon as we were safely in, they sped off with a wave goodbye. A small island lay just inside the reef and as it was close to sundown, we decided to anchor there and go on to the public landing the next day.

When we arose in the morning, we found the boat completely covered with large black flies. These flies were different than I had ever seen as they simply would not shush. Luckily we had our hatches covered with mosquito screens for the night and this infestation was confined to the exterior of the boat. Finally after brushing off all the flies, we sailed on around the island to the public landing area.

After anchoring next to a small loading dock, I put up our quarantine flag. This flag is an internationally recognize request for assistance in clearing customs and immigration. It happened to be Sunday so I was not surprised when there was no response to our request. Later in the afternoon, a young man swam out and climbing aboard our boat introduced himself as Simioni, a Fijian immigrant who owned a restaurant up the road from the harbor. When he invited us to come ashore with him, I replied I could not leave the boat until I had gotten clearance from the authorities. He only laughed and said no one would care but I insisted on waiting. I could just see myself standing in front of a judge with the excuse, Simioni told me nobody cares.

Shortly after Simioni left, a small boat pulled alongside and a pretty young lady climbed aboard. Introducing herself as Jaclyn, she was a local French school teacher and self appointed welcoming committee for the Island. Her gregarious attitude told me this was going to be a very pleasant visit. I had to tell her also I would wait until tomorrow before leaving the boat.

Well the next day dawned with the arrival of a small inter-island freighter which started unloading at the dock. Still no officials responded to my presents. After spotting a white face among the native laborers unloading, I finally went ashore and asked him for assistance in contacting customs and immigration. He informed me that he was the customs agent and asked "Could you come by my office on Thursday?" Obviously he wasn't worried about my being a smuggler. He informed me there was no formal immigration department but I should just go up the hill behind the harbor and check in with the Gendarmes. Up the hill we went and while we were filling out the visitors form, the policeman suddenly exclaimed, "Mon Ami, this is your birthday!" This was a big surprise to me. I hadn't taken any sun sights since leaving Samoa and I had lost all track of the date.

This is a small island so word soon got around to Simioni and he caught up with us as we were walking back to the boat. His insistence on our presents at his restaurant for a birthday dinner set the tone for our visit here. We had a typical French dinner that evening with many separate courses finished off at the end with what was considered to be the ultimate dessert. Canned Peaches! This was my fiftieth Birthday and I can't recall ever having a more pleasant one.

The following day Jaclyn was back and insisted we should move the boat from this commercial location to an anchorage off the beach by her house on the other side of the island. This location was in a very pleasant well protected bay so we had no objections to the move.

So we were off to our new friend's location and approaching the beach, I noticed many dark shapes in the water. This was a sure sign of shallow water over coral heads. Wendy, being an expert swimmer, dove off the boat and swam in ahead of me and signaled what to avoid as we came closer to the shore. I finally spotted a bright blue area of sand bottom and I let go the anchor. This turned out to be an ideal spot for later, when the tide went out; the boat was completely surrounded by water shallow enough for wading ashore. This also provided me with another opportunity to refresh the bottom paint. I was later able to manually tow the boat high up on the beach at high tide and repaint the bottom when the tide went out.

We remained at this anchorage for the entire month we were on Wallis Island. One day we and our host peddled our bicycles on a very soggy road through the middle of the island to the opposite side. Having to stop frequently to clear the mud from between the wheels and the bicycle frame made this trip a one of a kind. She wanted to show us her school which was on that side and in spite of the mud; it was really worth the effort.

Two weeks after our arrival, Jaclyn flew to New Caledonia on holiday and on her invitation, we were treated to the run of her house for a week. It was there I recorded "Us and Them" from her Pink Floyd album. Twenty three years later, I still have that cassette and playing it still can recreate for me the wonderful experience of that time and place.

We were still relying on our boat stores for most of our food, but for variety in our diet we frequently trekked off the road into the bush looking for wild banana and papaya. The local Catholic Nuns kept us supplied with eggs and French bread. We also ate the locally available produce of taro, breadfruit and cassava. Try as I might though, I could never see any profit in eating breadfruit. This abomination is the pithy seed pod of a small tropical tree which more closely resembles?? ----- well I know of nothing on earth which it closely resembles. I tried every conceivable way of cooking and seasoning it but in spite of all my efforts, it successfully resisted every attempt I made to turn it into food. And to think the English were planning on using it to feed their slaves in the Caribbean. I am sure this was an additional reason for the uprising which overthrew the colonial power.

A small store catering to the French offered a little more variety but everything having to be flown in on small single engine planes from New Caledonia, made it very expensive. Being desperate however, I once paid five dollars for a single cabbage.

When we first arrived and inquired about getting some fruit and vegetables, I was told there wasn't a market on the island. I asked in disbelief how could I get whatever produce was available and was told "Well, just ask someone." I guess you can't sell what every one is giving away. To illustrate the typical Island attitude about ownership of nature's bounty, I relate this example. Our host would have to closely watch her palmetto tree when the fruit was ripe because occasionally teenagers would help themselves. When she admonished them for stealing; their reply was "We're not stealing. We're only eating." In this island culture, I guess stealing meant removing and selling. If you consumed what you took, there was nothing wrong in that.

The two concessions to the modern world that existed here were a movie theater and a small Disco club.

On Simioni's, insistence we went to the movies with him and this was a very unique experience. The movie was in French and it would occasionally stall, plunging the theater into complete blackness. One time after a break, the movie resumed only now the picture was upside-down. I understood a little French from my Navy days but this was totally unintelligible to me. I apologized to Simioni for not being able to understand and he answered, "Don't feel bad. I can't understand it either" and he spoke fluent French.

Finally after a month, with great reluctance, we bade goodbye to this wonderful friendly place and again headed south.

Our next destination was Fatuna Island. Also governed by the French, it is much smaller than Wallis and has no off shore barrier reef. Only a narrow bay on the lee side is available for anchorage.

The people here were relatively unaccustomed to visitors and welcomed us with open arms. In fact a small argument ensued to see which family would have the privilege of being our host. The housing here was typical island, open walled and thatched roof architecture. Pigs roamed freely about the island and would forage for shell fish on the exposed reefs at low tide. These animals were as friendly as dogs and would, like a dog, watch closely for anything editable that might accidentally fall to the ground.

The locals cooked their bananas, taro and fish in a preheated pit in the ground in the evening and after digging it up in the morning, stored it in baskets hanging around their house. Eating was a casual affair with, as far as I could see, no formal times observed. If you were hungry you would just forage through the food baskets and take whatever looked good at the moment. Sleeping accommodations were nothing more than mats spread on the coral floor and if it rained, similar mats would be unrolled and hung to create a protective wall. Being relatively close to the Equator, this was only to avoid getting wet and not for protection from the cold.

They had a limited supply of electricity provided by a diesel generator that only ran until ten o'clock at night.

After ten it got really dark.

The most obvious evidence of outside influence was the bakery. This consisted of an earthen oven fired with coconut husks which baked the bread dough mixed in a dugout canoe which was no longer seaworthy. This was absolutely the best French bread I have ever tasted. The pigs liked it too, evidenced by the one who stole a loaf from my backpack lying on the ground while I was launching my dingy. I gave chase and recovered my bread but not wanting to eat after a pig, I gave it to my host to feed to their chickens. She however, brushed the sand off and after toasting it in their fire, fed it to her children.

There was a small hospital here on the island and here an unusual event occurred. Our host family had a gravely ill uncle in this hospital and they insisted on Wendy accompanying them on their daily visit. She reluctantly went with them and then upon her return, I noticed she was visibly upset. Her tearful explanation was, "Other people get invited to weddings or birthdays but I got invited to a death." It seems that the uncle actually died while they were visiting him.

This happening launched a ritual practiced by many islanders. Pigs were not routinely killed and eaten, and would be only in connection with a birth or a death. I imagined if the pigs could talk they would have sent out the word, "Run for the hills. Someone has just died."

I witness an absolutely hilarious scene when, in preparation for the funeral feast, one of the deceased's nephews came walking up the road carrying two small kicking and squealing pigs suspended on a line at each end of a pole across his shoulders. He was doing a sort of dance alternating between walking and kicking at the dogs running alongside, barking and snapping at the hapless pigs. It was a sort of step, step, kick, step, step, kick routine he was dancing. I really regretted not having a movie camera at that moment.

After a week of funeral ritual, when things returned to normal, I decided to contract strep throat. It is a real misery how one gets something like that in the middle of the ocean far away from civilization. I had a high fever for a day but after getting a high dosage shot of penicillin from the French Doctor at their small hospital, I was back on my feet just in time to be moving on again. Our friends here begged us to stay and even promised to build us a house on the beach if we did. This is not as big a deal as it might seem because their houses are simple pole and palm frond structures and here on this island, all their houses are on the beach.

Now the Fiji Islands lay ahead of us. The people of the nation of Fiji are about evenly divided between indigenous Fijian natives and immigrant Asian Indians. The latter brought in by the early English Colonial government to work in the sugar industry. Even though they are all equal citizens of the country, individuals are always referred to as either Fijian or Indian. There was very little assimilation by the people in these two cultures who, for the most part, followed their individual customs of food and dress. This provided an interesting choice for any visitor lucky enough to be there.

Reading the sailing instructions, I found the two Ports Of Call in Fiji were located far inside the island group. This meant we would have to sail past many of the outer islands without stopping and check in at either the capital, Suva on the main island of Viti Levu or the former capital Lavuka, on the smaller island of Ovalou. We entered the island cluster and sailed all night and most of the next day when, as the sun was setting, the wind direction became favorable for making Lavuka our destination. Sailing up between the main island of Viti Levu on the left and a large reef system on the right made navigating in the dark somewhat unnerving. The waterway here was plenty wide but it had no navigable exit at the far end and if I failed to see the port of Lavuka, I could go on the reef in the dark. The atmosphere was very strange that night. There seemed to be a faint orange glow in the air but I was unable to distinguish a single form of any kind. Usually at night on the ocean, the stars provide enough illumination to see a faint horizon and other features like mountains. This night I could not see anything at all. There was nothing I could do but carry on the best I could. I shortened sail and ghosted along all night using only a compass heading for navigation and just before dawn, I was greatly relieved when I saw the harbor lights at Lavuka materialize in the distance.

The Harbor Master here was Indian and very friendly and helpful. Wendy phoned her parents in California to let them know we had arrived safely.

Lavuka was the original capital of Fiji but as it was virtually a single street town with the main thoroughfare running for its full length next to the water; the capital was later moved to Suva.

This is a quaint small town which I liked very much. All the stores were located on the mountain side of the street and being completely human size could easily be covered from one end to the other on foot.

After a week in Lavuka, we sailed around to Suva and anchored in the bay next to the Tradewinds Hotel. The Tradewinds was a popular destination for cruising boats for it provided at a modest price, mail delivery, hot water showers, car parking and a secure dingy landing. One memorable event happened while we were here at this location. I was hauling my dingy up onto the dock and I noticed another dingy with several men approaching. One of the occupants was talking and I immediately knew I had heard that voice before. The face that went with the voice didn't look familiar at first but after I looked closer, I finally realized who it was. There was no mistaking the voice of Mark Twain. Of course I am referring to Hal Holbrook. He had the questionable advantage of having someone else sail his boat to Fiji and I heard him say he had to fly back to the US and go to work. Going to work was the last thing on my mind.

Not having any real plans for the future, Wendy and I just lived day to day; doing whatever prompted us at the moment. We would usually make a trip to the large open market in Suva to buy fresh fruit and vegetables. The interesting way the venders there would display and sell their produce, I believe was unique to Fiji. Produce like bananas, cassava, eggplant, green beans, etc, were displayed and sold "by the heap." A number of piles, each called a heap, were displayed. When one heap was sold, a single item each from the remaining heaps would be removed and a new heap created so as time wore on, the number of heaps remained constant but the size of each got smaller. If buying by the heap, it paid to shop early. I really liked this market because it had so many different things on display. There was a variety of fresh fish, different kinds of shellfish, fruits, vegetables, and every spice imaginable for compounding the different varieties of curries the Indians use in their cooking.

One of the quaint customs here in Fiji was a breakfast of boiled egg, sweet bun with butter and tea offered at many of the varied shops. And speaking of quaint, a big item in the Fiji Sun one day was the story of a young man who had been fined twenty five dollars for stealing a boiled egg.

Downtown Suva sported everything one could want in a developed country. Numerous clothing and general merchandise stores lined the streets. Indian music leaked out of many of the stores and if you didn't look Fijian or Indian, you would be occasionally solicited on the street in an attempt to lure you into one of the many specialty shops. The City boasted four movie theaters showing American and British productions plus a few smaller ones playing exclusively Indian Movies. Many English and Indian eateries as well as Fish and Chip and Chinese restaurants were also well represented. We frequently went to the movies and I thought their pricing and seating arrangements were unique. All the large theaters were built with main floor and balcony seating. I always thought the balcony was the cheap seats but here they were reversed. Eighty cents got you a seat with the wealthy in the balcony and fifty cents put you with the rabble below. Paying the higher price still wouldn't protect you from having to watch a movie with the reels occasionally shown out of sequence. This out of sequence showing happened to me once during the presentation of John Wayne's movie Hatari. I had previously seen it so I knew how it was suppose to run but no one else seemed to notice or mind.

Fiji has an excellent public transportation system but needing more independence, I decided to buy a small 125 CC motorcycle.

This was the highest horsepower motorcycle allowed in the country and Wendy and I rode it everywhere. We managed to ride the partially unsealed road along the coast and through the foothills from Suva to Lautoka. This road was called unsealed because for half of its length it was paved with loose stones. These stones would, over time; all get thrown to the side of the road by the passing traffic. Periodically then, these scattered stones would be redistributed back upon the road with a mechanical road scrapper. The fact that some of these stones could be as large as golf balls, made riding a motorcycle on this surface quite interesting. On one trip, the front wheel stopped when it sank into an area of loose stone flipping us over the handlebars. I landed on the road with Wendy on top of me. I just got skinned up a little but Wendy luckily escaped completely unhurt. After straightening up the handlebars we were off again, miraculously more embarrassed than hurt.

The bridge across the Sigatoka River next to the town of Sigatoka presented another interesting problem. This bridge was only one vehicle wide and a lot of cooperation was needed to ensure everyone got their turn crossing.

Deciding to see more of the country from the boat, we sailed down the coast past Sigatoka and anchored in the bay next to the Fijian Hotel. We were a part of a small flotilla welcomed by the hotel. Their feeling was having a group of yachts in their bay gave the place a look of exclusiveness. We had access to all their public facilities and we took advantage of most of them. The only negative was their beer prices were a little high for our limited resources. From here we would ride the bus to Sigatoka and buy our supplies at their native market. Across the street from this market was a small Indian eatery which served the best curry I have ever tasted. This place was basic plywood furniture without menus or decor. While we were eating in there one day, a tourist couple from New Zealand came in and ordered fish and chips. The owner stated, "We got lamb curry, goat curry, and vegetable curry. No fish and chips." I tried to get these people to try some of the curries but they were unwilling to experiment. I never understood why anyone would not at least try something new. I haven't always liked everything I tried but I was always willing to take a chance.

One day a small tragedy happened while returning from one of our trips to the market. We were walking from the road across the bridge to the Hotel and Wendy was carrying a dozen eggs we had bought. A sudden gust of wind blew open the wraparound skirt she was wearing and she immediately spun around to close her skirt and in so doing, sent the eggs flying. We had been watching our money closely and even a small thing like loosing those eggs affected her all out of proportion to what it should have. I assured her things like that happen. She initially wanted to try and salvage what we could but that was beyond doing.

After a couple of weeks at The Fijian Hotel we set out to see some of the other islands south of Viti Levu.

My favorite, Lavuka, happened to be on the way to our next destination and we just couldn't sail right on past without stopping for a little visit. While anchored there this time, we met the proprietors of the Royal Hotel and I heard they were planning to take their work boat to Suva for supplies. After some broad hinting, I managed to get invited along for the ride.

We left Lavuka long before sunup and swung around the Island through the inland passage between Ovalau and Viti Levu. In the cool morning darkness, the house maid riding along with us offered me a cup of something which was hot and very sweet. After I finished drinking, I asked the girl to serve my coffee black in the future and she replied there was no coffee available. What she had given me was tea. There had been so much sugar and milk in it; I couldn't detect any taste of tea.

At daylight, I could see we were entering the mouth of a river which I found, wound mile after mile up into Viti Levu's interior. After coming onto and taking different forks, I noticed we were no longer motoring upstream but now strangely, down stream. Then to my amazement we exited the mouth of the Rewa River into Laucala Bay right next to Suva. We had motored up one river to its headwaters which joined the headwaters of another and exited at the mouth of the second one. There may be other river systems like this somewhere on earth but I have never heard of one. This was not a mile wide Mississippi type of river and was no wider than fifty feet in places.

Supplies loaded, we returned to Lavuka the way we had

come and I paid particular attention to the landscape for I was hatching an idea to be used in the future.

A day after I returned to Lavuka, we set sail for Taveuni. This is a large Island and almost completely covered with Coconut Palms. Very sparsely populated, it was a wonderful place for hiking and we took full advantage of the opportunity.

We spent the next two weeks sight seeing through the many bays and inlets of this island which resembled a movie set.

While we were at anchor off the town of Somo Somo one afternoon, a small power boat full of bananas, coconuts, breadfruit and papaya pulled alongside and inquired if we eat any of these things. When I replied we did, he began unloading everything as fast as he could. I stopped him saying we could not eat that much and it would only spoil. His reply was "So what? It will spoil on the beach anyway."

One day we realized we were getting low on our boat's supply of fresh water and with the aid of a friendly local copra planter, we hiked up a mountain stream with empty five gallon containers looking for a spring where our guide assured us the water would be safe. Finding a likely spot, we brushed aside the floating leaves and filled our jugs. This was the kind of independent living I really enjoyed.

Another day we rode from his plantation to Savu Savu town on his truck loaded with copra being taken to market. Wendy rode in front with the driver and I gladly rode in back laying on the load; all the while chewing on dried coconut pieces. The return trip however was not so enjoyable. I now shared the back with two fifty five gallon drums of kerosene. The rough rutted road created a vibration which caused the unsecured drums to erratically chase me around making sitting down impossible even if I had wanted to. The trucks motion, in addition to the smell of kerosene, made me a little ill. Some times one must have a little discomfort in order to really appreciate the good times but there should be limits.

Returning to Suva we stopped at Lavuka for the third time. I decided I wanted to try sailing back to Suva following the same course I previously had taken in the Hotel's work boat. We left Lavuka in the late morning and by the time I got through the inboard passage to the river's mouth; it was too late in the afternoon to try to make it through before dark so I anchored where I was. Here I observed a strange sight that seems to be unique to Fiji. In the distance I saw what looked to me to be around ten people in a row gliding past waist deep in the water. Getting out my binoculars, I discovered they all were sitting in a very long, narrow canoe with a motor on the back. The canoe was so low in the water it was almost invisible. What made it even stranger was they all were dressed fit to go to church.

Early the next morning we started up the river. I had some anxious moments when coming to the various forks, being uncertain if I was remembering the correct one. We were motoring through farm land broken only by an occasional small cluster of houses. Frequently we were greeted with much waving and shouting by children playing on the river banks. The river's meander was so sharp at times we could see another boat across the land apparently going in the opposite direction but it was actually behind us in the part of the river we had just left. After we got into the headwaters, navigation was easier because all I had to do was follow the current downstream. We finally made it safely into Laucala Bay where we immediately went aground in the mud. Luckily it was at low tide and when the flow reversed we were able to continue on to our mooring at the Tradewinds.

There was one more place I wanted to visit while in Fiji. Years before in Hawaii, I had purchased a book with pictures of many exotic looking places in the South Pacific and I had planned to visit as many of them as I could. One picture taken from the top of a hill overlooking the beach of a small island looked particularly appealing to me. This Island was located south of Viti Levu in the Astrolabe lagoon. This large lagoon contained dozens of small islands making finding the right one quite a challenge. Using the picture in my book as a reference, I was able to find the same pattern of islands on my chart and locate the one I wanted. I anchored my boat in the exact spot shown in the picture. I even climbed the hill and stood where the previous photographer had stood. This was a very fulfilling experience for me. I knew looking at pictures can create a very false impression of the scene but except for the fact I was a little warm and sweaty, my experience of this scene was as I had imagined it would be. A deep blue watery expanse, broken only by dark green images of other small islands in the distance, lay before me. This view was exactly the same as the one I saw in my book.

A very false idea about the luxury of having a tropical island of your own has been created by writers sitting in air conditioned spaces with cold drinks close at hand. The reality is somewhat different. To begin with, all of the smaller islands have no fresh water available. Even if there is a small stream, water flows only for a short time after a rain. This single fact is the reason hundreds of these islands are uninhabited.

My brother and I had talked many times about what it would be like to be sitting under a palm tree on a sandy beach where your footprints were the only ones visible. There would be a gentle breeze rustling the palm fronds over your head and the only other sound was the surf caressing the sand at your feet.

Well I was exactly in such a place. Looking around I thought. This is it. Yes! This is it. -------This is it???? Man, after a bit, this is really boring. I am sticky with salt from sweat and the sea air. It is uncomfortable hot and the sand fleas are biting my ass. Oh what I wouldn't give to be having a cold beer in a nice air-conditioned bar right now."

I am sorry to have disillusioned you but that is how it really is sometimes.

Wendy and I had by now been in Fiji for almost a year and we decided to fly back to California for a visit with a stopover in Hawaii. In California, Wendy and I agreed to separately visit our respective friends and relatives and I would return to Fiji ahead of her as I didn't like leaving the boat unattended for any longer than necessary. On my way back, I was at a friend's house in Hawaii when Wendy called and told me she was not going to return to Fiji. I was completely stunned by this news. Our relationship had been close and intimate for over six years. She had been my loving and enthusiastic other half for all of that time. We had discussed getting married on many occasions but we hadn't because she wanted me to "want" to be married and as I had been married so many times before, I was only willing to rather than desirous. As I knew from experience, a marriage contract was no guarantee to a successful lifelong relationship and I thought a daily commitment was the ultimate proof of love.

I suppose I could have tried to change her mind but at the moment I was quite hurt and all I could say was "Well, you have do what you have to do."

I never knew what happened on her visit with her family and can only guess why she made that decision. Even if we had been married, we wouldn't have been able to have any children and perhaps she felt the need for more. Maybe her family convinced her she was in a relationship they thought was going nowhere. Or maybe she, as I had in the past, felt a need to look for something else.

I never pressed her for an explanation.

Back in Fiji without Wendy, my life changed a lot. Naturally, I missed her very much. One of the most difficult things for me was eating alone. Trying to eat on the boat was particularly difficult because of the constant reminder of Wendy's absents.

Luckily for me, Wendy and I had become good friends with a New Zeeland couple anchored next to us at the Tradewinds. Ross and Marita always made me welcome on their boat and now it helped to have someone to talk with. They were surprised but not judgmental and completely neutral in their reaction to Wendy's decision.

It was at this time I also became friends with Peter, the Fijian guitar player in the combo playing nightly in the Hotel lounge. Knowing I was alone, he invited me to his house every evening after he had finished playing. We would stop on the way and buy some "Grog." This was the powdered root of the yongona plant which, when mixed with water, made a muddy looking, bad tasting, slightly narcotic drink that is the staple mood altering drink of Fijian society. Peter was an interesting person who, even though he was Fijian, had been raised among Indians and had a close association with their culture. When our conversations got around to girls, he would always recommend marring an Indian instead of a Fijian. His observation was, "All Fijian girls do is smoke, drink, and they eat like hogs." I think he had a somewhat slanted view. After several hours of drink and conversation, I would somewhat wobbly, ride my motorcycle back to the boat.

Grog was so commonly consumed in Fiji, it could be found everywhere. There was even a communal bowl in the lobby of the bank. About three o'clock every afternoon in the market and elsewhere, all activity stopped and the grog bowls were brought out. The common economical version was the pre-processed powered form which only required mixing with water before consuming. This form was available everywhere. Less common was the brew made directly from the plant root. One night Peter's wife mixed a supply for us using the root as her source and not being familiar with its effect, I consumed my usual amount. At about three in the morning I was going to the bathroom on my hands and knees. Walking had become impossible. After about three hours sleep, I managed to get on my motorcycle and miraculously made it back to my boat. As this is an organic compound and not volatile like alcohol, the effects do not dissipate quickly. It took an entire week for its effects to completely disappear. The lasting result is I have a permanent revulsion for the stuff.

As part of my newly acquired bachelor status, I discovered the best place to have lunch in Suva was in the YWCA. Here they served up a generous plate of vegetable curry with Roti (Indian bread resembling Mexican flour Tortillas) for only eighty cents. The ingredients in the curry would change depending on what was available and cheap at the market the previous day. It could be any mixture of green bean, potato, egg plant, or pumpkin (squash) but always vegetable.

Time passed and one afternoon while resting below in my boat, I heard a thud on the side and investigating, met a burly looking man in a dingy hanging onto the railing. Seeing me, he inquired if I was the person who was rumored to know about electronics. I replied that all depended on what was required. It seems he needed someone to look at the Radar on his small freighter tied up in the harbor. I said I'd have a look at it and went with him. I spent every day for an entire week on his ship. I was able to repair his radar which only needed a new crystal and

I designed a twenty four volt battery charger for him. His cook would make a nice lunch for everyone and in the late afternoon, he would send one of the crew into town to bring back a case of quart size bottles of Fiji Bitter beer. We would spend the evening on his ship, drinking beer and watching the local hookers trying to seduce the Korean fishermen on the boats next to us. No one had mentioned payment of any kind and I didn't expect any as I was enjoying myself and with lunch and beer in the evening, what more could one want. At the end of the week, he came by and stuffed a wad of bills in my hand. Sorting them out later, I counted two hundred dollars American. This money came in at the right time as I was getting very close to the bottom of my reserves.

I was now again without a crew and to make matters worse, I was informed that I would have to pay an import fee if my boat remained in Fiji longer than one year. Coincidentally, Intelect, my old employer back in Hawaii, had sent me a wire asking me to return and set up and operate the new design computer they were purchasing. I had always remained in contact with them and I had periodically submitted invoices for money they owed me when I left on my adventure. This account had by now been exhausted and I was nearly broke.

The idea of trying to sail all the way back to Hawaii alone was a little frightening but not totally out of the question. There had been only a couple of times when Wendy's help was essential and if I had been alone I would have taken more precautions.

I now thought I would do something a little crazy so I placed an ad for a "Sailing Lady" in the Fiji Sun newspaper.

This ad simply stated, "Wanted; One Sailing lady to crew on a trip to Hawaii and the US." Surprisingly, I got a lot of responses but before I started interviewing the most likely sounding ones, I shaved off my full beard and mustache of six years. Wendy had never complained about it as she was a natural type girl who didn't shave anywhere either. This was a wise move now.

All the responses I received from Indian ladies were with the assumption they would expect to be married. This is not as strange as it seems as arranged marriages were and still are common in Indian culture. Marring someone you hardly know is not seen as something to be avoided at all costs.

I was fifty one years old at the time so I eliminated most of the nineteen year old applicants. In the Indian culture, all girls should be married by the time they reach nineteen, so if not married by then, they stopped getting any older. It would be difficult to determine how old some of these "nineteen" year old girls really were. Many of the letters I received moved me deeply as they expressed a sort of pleading desperation with an additional "You won't be sorry" promise.

I was severely tempted by one young lady. She was absolutely beautiful and willing to get married. Like a moth to a flame, I visited her at her home three times and allowed myself the titillating fantasy of being married to her. However finally drawing on what little moral integrity I had left, I could not in good conscience have married her for she was only nineteen years old and thirty two years my junior. I was almost old enough to be her Grandfather.

As the result of a phone call I made to another applicant, two young Fijian girls met me at the Tradewinds. I rowed them out to the boat and we sat exchanging pleasantries for about an hour. When I delivered them back to the Hotel, one of them claimed she had left her belt on the boat and would I take her back to retrieve it. I said it would be faster if I rowed back alone and get it for her. Returning to the boat, I was unable to find anything and when I looked back at the Hotel, they both were gone. I can only guess what this young lady's motive was for wanting to return to my boat without her friend. She may have initially brought her friend along as a safety precaution and after sizing me up, decided to have another go at it alone.

Another respondent in particular, interested me because her letter came with postage due. After paying the missing one cent due at the post office, I called the telephone number in the enclosed letter and after introducing myself; asked to speak to Anila. All I heard at first was muffled voices in the background. Finally I heard a female voice say hello. I didn't know it at the time but Anila's younger sister Usha, had seen my ad and answered it signing Anila's name. When I called of course she knew nothing about what her sister had done and was understandably mystified. However after much urging by Usha, she hesitantly started talking to me. After I explaining what this was all about, she agreed to meet me. Our date was set for the following evening in the lobby of the YWCA.

The next day when I arrived, I was a little concerned to find a large group of young girls milling about in the lobby and not having agreed to wear some sort of identifying item, it was impossible for me to identify my date. I was the only male in the crowd so she could have assumed I was it but scanning the many faces I didn't detect a single look of interest. After a time the crowd thinned out until finally everyone had left except the two of us. We looked at each other rather suspiciously. She did not meet my expectations and I certainly did not fit the image she had in her mind. I finally, hesitantly went over and asked "Are you Anila?" She nodded and after introducing myself, I suggested we walk up the street to the local Chinese Restaurant where we could sit and talk.

She seemed very shy and hesitant so I did most of the talking at first. Relaxing a bit, she told me she was thirty two years old, unmarried and a school teacher. She also informed me everyone in her family called her Ani instead of Anila. I tried to be as charming as I could and started thinking I should see more of her if possible. When we left the restaurant I insisted on taking her home in a Taxi. I knew that way I could find out where she lived. On the ride to her home, I asked if I could come tomorrow to meet her family. She agreed but said she would be teaching at school until three o'clock and wouldn't be home before that.

On our way back to the YWCA to get my motorcycle, my taxi driver asked me, "Are you going to marry that girl?" He had overheard our conversation about our meeting and I thought he was about to give me some needed advice about the type of girls who frequented the park next to the YWCA. I of course knew all about these girls and when I started to explain, he interrupted me, saying he knew Ani's brother who also was a taxi driver and he assured me this was a good family.

The next afternoon found me in the front room of her house with the women of the family giggling and peering at me through a slit in the kitchen wall. She was not home yet so this was a rather uncomfortable time with no one saying anything. Luckily she arrived in time to introduce me to her father and brothers. Her father was an interesting man who had been around a bit and I soon found we had much in common. Their family background was very much like mine and I was surprised to find there seems to be a universal experience enjoyed by all farmers regardless of the ethnic or geographic background.

They insisted I stay for supper and had a laugh at my expense when I didn't know how to eat curry using only my right hand without the assistance of utensils. I found eating dal (a kind of lintel soup) with roti to be the most challenging.

The following day was Saturday and I again was at her house. In the afternoon we rode to the Tradewinds and I introduced her to the boat. While there, she insisted on washing my clothes. She was starting out on the right foot. We returned to her house in time for dinner and spent the evening watching Hindi movies. The Indian custom of the sexes being separated in social settings was practiced at her home, so while watching the movie, all the females sat on one side of the room and all the males sat on the other. Ani and I managed to be at the dividing line between the sexes and sat on the couch next to each other while holding hands behind our backs. I don't think we were fooling anyone.

These visits became a regular event and on the fourth day in the morning, I stopped by Ross's boat for breakfast and brought them up to date on my latest activities. They had wanted a daily report on all my interviews and I told them about Ani and when asked about how I felt, I answered "I think I'm beginning to really like this girl."

Later that afternoon, I picked Ani up and brought her out to the boat again. We talked into the evening and just before taking her home, I asked if she would like to sail with me. She said she would but her parents would not agree unless we were married. Knowing being married was not fatal, I had no objections. It was about eleven o'clock when she got home and her brother raised a fuss asking what the neighbors might think with her coming in at that late hour. Even at the age of thirty two she could not escape the strong fundamental beliefs of her culture.

Time for me to be out of the country was getting short so we set about getting married as soon as possible. In Fiji, civil ceremonies are performed separate from the Hindu wedding rituals and we decided to get the former done first.

While applying for the civil permit in Suva, I was asked if I had previously been married. Not being one to lie, I answered yes. Now I was told I would have to produce proof I was divorced. I though this was the most absurd requirement imaginable. If I had told the truth about having been married, why would I lie about being divorced? It would have been much simpler to have just lied about being previously married in the first place.

Well we blew it in Suva but luckily there was another place we could tie the knot. With Ani's father and mother in tow, we drove to the town of Lautoka on the other side of the island. There, when asked about previous marriages, I just lied and said none. They might have thought it a bit strange that a fifty one year old never married American bachelor was marring a thirty two old never married Indian spinster but no one said anything. Perhaps what made the difference was fact that the Judge who married us was an old schoolmate of the bride's father.

Anila Devi Datt was now Anila Devi Hoff
We spent the first night of our marriage in a small tourist hotel and before retiring to our room we sat with other guests in the lobby and watched the Peter Sellers movie, There's a Girl in My Soup. By some strange coincidence, this was the same movie playing when I had stayed in this Hotel before. Thinking about it now, maybe that was the only movie they had and as no one went there more than once, they didn't need another one.

Back in Suva we had a traditional Hindu Wedding which, given the time constraints, was abbreviated quite a bit from the usual three day event. The entire ceremony was performed in Hindi so I understood nothing of what was being said but Ani's aunt translated the parts I needed to know in order for me to make the correct moves. In spite of its brevity, our wedding was a very colorful and festive affair.

## Author and Ani on their Wedding Day

When my friend Ross had earlier asked me if I was going to marry this girl, I answered, "What the hell, this is just one more thing no one from Holgate has ever done."

Unlike Christian ceremonies, the Hindu versions are a lot less formal with children running around and playing through. Also many symbolic items like flower petals, rice, yogurt, and other assorted leaves are required and if something happens to be missing or unsatisfactory, everything stops until the appropriate corrections are made. I was all decked out with charcoal eye liner and turmeric on my body. This was the type of experience I really enjoy.

We now set about getting what we would need for our trip to Hawaii. Ani had to give two weeks notice on her teaching job in order to withdraw her retirement money. I took her to her school every day on the motorcycle and I can only imagine what her students thought when they saw their old maid school teacher throw her leg over the motorcycle seat behind me. This was good practice for her because motorcycles would be our only transportation for years in the future.

Finally, after a tearful wave goodbye to her family standing dockside at the Tradewinds, we were on our three thousand mile sail to Hawaii. I can only imagine how her family must have felt watching her sail off into the unknown with a man they had first met less than two weeks before.

I had wanted to retrace the original course I used sailing to Fiji and stop on Wallis Island but contrary winds and currents made sailing in that direction too uncomfortable. Sailing on a more northerly course for fifteen days brought us to the Tuvalu Islands. After anchoring next to the government pier on the main island of Funa Futi, we had a little trouble convincing the immigration officer we were really married and legal. Originally their customs agent had been aboard the boat with the immigration officer but then returned later without his friend to relieve us of several bottles of Fiji Bitter beer in return for a guided tour of the Island. I still cringe at the memory of him opening the beer bottles with his teeth. Ani used this opportunity to call her folks in Fiji and let them know we were safe.

I have never seen a place as dangerously close to the water as some parts of this island were. At one point, the road was on a strip of land only about fifty feet wide and only three feet above the high tide line. With the lagoon on one side and the Pacific ocean on the other, it sure didn't look like a good place to be if a Hurricane or Tsunami was eminent.

After only four days rest here, we were back at sea again. Now life became a daily routine of eating, sleeping and watching the waves constantly forming and passing in an unbroken repetitious cycle. My self steering gear worked so well I never had to touch it except to make small course changes. When the opportunity presented itself, I would chase small local showers and catch rain to keep our water tanks full. I had made for this very purpose, a tarp with a hose attachment at its center and it worked so well we were never in any danger of running out of water.

Infrequently we would get completely becalmed and the ocean would go totally flat without a ripple to be seen. During one such time, we were surrounded in the far distance by a few fishing boats which, unmoving, appeared like paintings on the horizon. During such calms, we would put our shade tarp over the deck and Ani would use the opportunity to make Curry and Roti. This spicy Indian food was always a welcome break from our usual canned fare.

Evenings were often spent lying in our berth listening to my short-wave radio. While slowly turning across the dial I would try to identify the stations as I came to them. While close to the Equator, I was able to get clear reception of many stations on the AM dial. New Zealand, Australia, California, and Hawaii came in perfectly clear and I always enjoyed listening to the Pidgin-english broadcasts from Papua New Guinea.

Lying in our berth in the daytime, sometimes we would be alerted to the presence of dolphins. The sound of their high frequency clicking was easily recognizable and going on deck, we could always see them broaching as they swam by. Not all life in the ocean lives in gregarious groups like the dolphins. The loneliest sight for me is an albatross forever gliding on the updraft of a wave front as it passes in front of the boat and disappears out of sight over the horizon. One bird all alone in a limitless expanse of sky and water. And speaking of lonely places, one afternoon I spotted what looked like surf ahead and slightly to our right. I hadn't been taking sun-sights routinely as I knew we were a long way from anywhere and had no fear of hitting anything. Looking at my chart I couldn't see anything like an island near us. As we got closer it became apparent this definitely was an island we were approaching. Not visible from any distance as it was nothing more than a sandy coral outcrop a few feet out of the water with absolutely nothing alive on it. Not one tree or blade of grass. If we had come onto it in the night and became marooned, this would have been indeed the loneliest place on earth. At first it seemed strange to see what was probably the very top of a sea mount. This reminded me of a question I would often get when in Hawaii. Thinking about sailing a long way away from land, many people think the ocean should be a lot rougher in the middle of the ocean so to speak. So when I would get that question, I would always answer with the observation that Hawaii is in the middle of the ocean and it is no worse here than anywhere else.

One day looking at our chart after an afternoon sun-sight, I realized we were still twelve hundred miles south of Hawaii and only six hundred miles north of Pago Pago. I had an unusual moment of impatience about our slow upwind progress and thought I would be better off turning around and heading south to Samoa. Acting on that impulse, I turned the boat around and after a few minutes of trying on the feeling of sailing south, sanity returned and I turned around again and resumed our northward course. I had to go through this exercise two more times before I could entirely give up the idea and remain on our original course to Hawaii. Part of my problem was the result of my sailing a direct route with no stopover islands along the way. This resulted in an overly long uninterrupted sameness which got pretty old. Some days when the ocean got a little rough, we wouldn't even bother to get out of our berths. This good old boat didn't mind carrying on alone and unattended.

The one bright spot in the otherwise dull routine was a daily treat I rationed out bit by bit. I had bought a quantity of hard candies in Suva and now I would give just one to Ani each day telling her to make her mouth happy. One day while performing this small ritual, I realized I was falling in love again. My reason for marrying Ani may have been I was on the rebound from losing Wendy but now I didn't care. I was absolutely sure I had done the right thing.

Just after dark on our fifty eighth day out of Suva, I spotted a faint glow in the sky on the distant horizon. Darn if my navigation didn't work again. The island of Oahu lay dead ahead.

Approaching the island, the seas became quite rough and seeing no profit in remaining on deck in the dark, I went below to the comfort of the interior. Knowing we were still quite far off and in no danger, I lay down and went to sleep. About three in the morning, I awoke with a feeling there was something wrong. It took me a moment to realize there was no longer much motion or sound. I stuck my head through the hatch and there we were, sailing smoothly along in the lee of the island about ten miles off the Waianae coast. Late morning found us anchored in my old home of Pokai Bay.

The proper thing to have done was to first land in Keehi and check in with immigration and customs but that was a long upwind sail and I had had enough of sailing for the moment. Instead, I chose to lay over and visit my old friend Jean-Louis here in Waianae. Luckily for us, we surprised them in the middle of preparing a barbeque on the beach. As I expected, Ani was immediately made part of the family but I however, was threatened with excommunication for not once contacting them during my entire two year sail south. At Jean-Louis's insistence, Ani called Fiji to let her family know she had arrived in Hawaii safely. I imagine they were pretty worried as it had been over forty five days since they had last heard from her.

After being at sea for two months, the experience of being on land, visiting with good friends and eating fresh food again was a little overwhelming and a real welcome change.

We rested there for the rest of that day and the next day sailed around to Keehi Lagoon and checked in with the customs and emigration.

# Chapter Five    Back In Hawaii

The first order of things after finding a good spot to anchor in Keehi Lagoon was going ashore and looking up all my old friends and catching up on more good things to eat. We walked up to Sizzlers in Kalihi where we accidentally ran into my friend Omar. He also hadn't seen or heard from me in over two years and here I was with a brand new sidekick in tow. Always being completely excepting of what people did, he welcomed Ani like one of the family. I was very lucky to have these kind of friends.

As my assets were by now reduced to a paltry forty dollars, the first order of business was to get a salary advance from Intelect. After lifting a thousand dollars from them and acquiring a cheap used motorcycle for transportation, I settled into my new job and Ani spent her days exploring her new home.

Ani's life in Fiji had been very different from what she would have to become accustomed to here. In Fiji she had never gone anywhere alone. She was always driven everywhere she went by her father or brother and if a bus was used, it would always be with the accompaniment of another responsible person. Now here, she had to manage on her own. One day I received a phone call from her telling me she was hopelessly lost and would I come and get her. She was calling from a service station just two blocks from my office. Prier to getting this close, she had ended up on the end of the bus line clear across the mountains on the other side of the island. But she was a fast learner and soon was managing very well by herself.

We continued to live on the boat in the Hawaiian style. When the weather was warm we would take a long walk along the beach and then have a bath in the public showers in Sand Island Park. These showers were quite invigorating as the water came, unheated, straight out of the mountains. In cooler weather we would heat a little water on the boat and after putting a tarp across the back of the cockpit for a shelter from the wind; take turns pouring water on each other. We could manage a bath using only half a gallon of water each.

About three months after our arrival in Hawaii, Ani received news that her father was quite ill. She immediately flew back to Fiji and then later when she tried to return to Hawaii, she was told her original visitor's visa could not be used and she would have to get an immigrant visa. This presented a series of obstacles the equal of which I had never before encountered. First I would have to make formal application for my wife's visa. This required that I prove we were legally married. Not knowing how deeply the department of immigration dug into ones past, I didn't want to try not being truthful about my divorces. I knew I was divorced by all my former wives but I had never gotten a single piece of paper to confirm it. Luckily I knew where they had all filed but I was a little hazy on when. So I wrote to the appropriate county department of records requesting any divorce records between myself and whoever on whatever dates. Much to my surprise, I got a timely response from all of them. This last hurdle overcome, I filed everything with immigration in Honolulu. I received a call several days later and was asked to come down for an interview. This was just to go over all my papers and at the end of the interview the agent smiling said "Mr. Hoff, everything looks fine and your wife should be back with you in six months." Six months??!! He explained everything would have to go to INS in Washington who would then notify the Embassy in Fiji, who would then notify Ani, who then would have to provide health and police records with her application.

Months later, I was standing outside the International Arrival Gate at the Honolulu Airport when I spotted a familiar face on a body completely different than I remembered. She had lost a lot of weight. Maybe this was the result of lugging along with her, a box the size of a small coffin filled with Fiji Bitter beer. It was really good to have her back where she belonged, with or without the beer.

Ani got a job with my old friend Omar the Tent Man and this made it possible for us to have lunch together every day. We would pick up a "Two Scoop Rice" plate lunch from one of the many purveyors on Canal Street and eat while sitting on the low wall at the edge of the Canal. Sitting there with Ani and watching the small fish darting around below, created such a sense of peace and contentment in me that I was always very reluctant to return to the office and work.

Over the years, Intelect moved locations several times and Ani had several different employers which always created some variety in our schedules. At one time, Ani worked as a sales clerk for a Philippine company and she became friends with many of her co-workers. This resulted in our being invited to many of their parties and one such invitation created a little drama. This event was a potluck affair and the plan was I should go to our boat after work and pick up a pot of Goulash and bring it to the party. On my way on my motorcycle, I was cut off by a car and went sprawling down the street. I was not badly hurt but did have a few skin abrasions. The motorcycle was not badly damaged so I was able to drive myself to the hospital emergency room where my wounds were cleaned and bandaged. I called Ani and said I might be a little late getting to the party but I didn't tell her why as she would have imagined it to be much worse than it really was. So when I walked into the room with blood seeping through the bandages, it created quite a scene.

Time passed and our routine varied little except during these years we made three visits to Ani's family in Fiji by hitch-hiking rides on Hawaiian Air deadhead flights. These were lucky times for us. Hawaiian Air had been contracted to rotate the Fijian Army troops assigned to UN duty in Lebanon. As the plane would be empty on the trip from Hawaii to Fiji and empty again on the return trip, they offered a ride at a very low price to anyone willing to leave Hawaii and return from Fiji on their schedule. This schedule would give us over a week in Fiji to visit family and friends. Usually these flights were only about one quarter full so one person could occupy an entire row of seats. This experience spoiled me completely and as a result flying any other way seems very cramped. Unfortunately, these flights were only available once a year.

Living on the boat did present me with unique problems. Ani had gone to Fiji for a month on a charter flight and I planned to join her after three weeks and we would fly home together a week later. I had purchased my round trip ticket on the same charter and my flight was scheduled to leave Hawaii at six thirty in the afternoon. On the morning of that day I received some very disheartening news. The weather forecasters were issuing a Hurricane warning for the Islands. I went to my office and kept listening to the radio for updates. It was uncertain exactly were this Hurricane might go and how intense it might be. I was in a real dilemma. If I got on the plane at six thirty not knowing if the boat would be safe, I wouldn't be able to sleep for a week. On the other hand if I waited until I knew the threat was over, I could lose my non refundable charter ticket.

What to do? As the day wore on and the time for a decision grew near, I was filled with a growing uncertainty. This was one of those situations in life when fate gives you only two options and neither one is acceptable. By five thirty, the news about the impending Hurricane still was not optimistic so I just gave up and decided to wait it out. Seven hours later, the Hurricane threat was canceled. Now I was really upset. So upset in fact I threw all reason to the winds and immediately caught the bus to the Airport. Scanning the projected departure flights, I spotted one on Quantus stopping in Fiji. Fortunately there were still some vacancies on that flight and using my Charter ticket for the return portion, I was able to get a one way ticket at the last minute. That one way fare cost me a little more than my Charter round trip ticket but I was determined not to miss out on this trip.

This drama was not over yet. Ani, in Fiji, had expected me to arrive in the morning on my original flight and when it came and I didn't, she started to panic. Calling my office in Hawaii, she was very relieved to learn I was on my way.

There were two other events of note which occurred while we were living on the boat in Keehi Lagoon. The first was the arrival of Hurricane Iva. On the morning of that day, I went to the office as usual and there I heard of the impending arrival of this wind. Its arrival was predicted to be later in the afternoon so I didn't return to the boat until lunch time. By then the wind had picked up quite a bit and I had a bit of trouble getting out to our boat which was anchored across the channel from the State Marina. Originally the wind was blowing parallel with the channel and everything seemed safe enough. I sat in the cockpit, being alert and ready for action in the event something went wrong. The possibility that my anchor would drag and I would drift into another boat was always real. In fact that is what almost happened. I didn't have enough anchor rope deployed to withstand the increased pull of the wind and I noticed we were getting closer to the boat behind us. Letting out a little more line to stop out drift would bring us dangerously close so I was forced to let out enough to drift completely past our neighbor and ended safely behind him. This extra line also gave the anchor a much better angle for gripping the bottom and we were now secure. I really wasn't too concerned at this point because if the boat did continue to drift there was nothing dangerous down wind from where we were and we would have just gone onto a sandy beach. As I had intentionally beached the boat many time before I knew this presented no problem. This was my first hurricane and I was learning on the fly. A little after dark, the wind started swinging around moving us closer to the channel. The waves generated here in this protected lagoon were not as high as I had encountered while sailing but the wind's steady howling was unnerving. As the storm moved, the wind direction continued to change and we were finally rotated until we were across the channel with my boat only about fifty feet from the boats bouncing in their births at the marina. Still sitting in the cockpit, I don't know what I would have done if my boat had broken lose at that time. I might have been able to glance off their sterns and end up in between them on the stone seawall. I was sitting there contemplating my possible moves when all the lights on the island went out. It was as though someone had thrown a switch. It was now eerily dark and this only intensified the uncertainty of the eventual outcome of this night. Finally at around midnight, I heard the wind give a final screech and then it abated ever so slightly. I had been in a state of extreme tension for over ten hours and now, with the assurance that if something was going to break it would have done so, I went below and crawled into my bed.

Awake at eight the next morning, I was greeted by the sun shining brightly in a deep blue sky with a warm gentle breeze rippling the water ever so slightly. Our boat was back in its normal place in the lagoon; just as though nothing had happened.

This was Thanksgiving Day, 1982.

Ani and I went ashore and rode our motorcycle around surveying the damage the hurricane had inflicted on the island. The storm had blown the High Tension electric lines down and much of the island was without power. Many trees were down across the roads and loose debris was everywhere. We had earlier received an invitation for Thanks Giving dinner with my long time employer so we rode over the mountain to keep our appointment with them. They had suffered no major damage but without electricity to heat anything, it was fortunate they had a charcoal grill and were able to make do with that. This was one of the most interesting Thanksgiving Dinners I ever experienced.

Another potentially devastating possibility in the Islands is the arrival of Tidal Waves. As a result of several earlier experiences with their destructive power, these forces were taken very seriously by the locals and an island wide early warning system was created.

And so it was one day when an earthquake in the South Pacific somewhere created a Tidal Wave alert here in Hawaii. Its time of arrival was determined several hours in advance and everyone was told to literally head for the hills. The radio was constantly warning the public to leave the beaches and low lying areas. Reporters were stationed on the Hotel roofs with long lens cameras to record the event. We in the boating community were advised to put to sea where a tidal wave presents no real danger. I elected to remain at anchor where I was because I believed the large reef system guarding our anchorage would be able to dissipate most of wave's energy and we would only feel a strong surge. As the afternoon wore on with an unbroken stream of boats still in the process of exiting the lagoon, the appointed time of the wave's arrival came and went without incident. I confess I was a little disappointed. We could have had at least a small Tidal Wave that would have done no damage but would have put a little excitement in out lives. It was later reported the wave was only six inches in height.

After about four years, Ani got a little tired of life on the boat and as we had saved a bit of money, we started looking for better accommodations on land.

Luckily we found a two bedroom condominium in the Makaha Valley Plantation that we both liked and before I knew what happened, I was no longer a sailor but a property owner with a small mortgage.

This was an extreme change for me. I had lived completely debt free for the preceding ten years and the thought of having to make mortgage payments was a little frightening. I hadn't realized it but not being financially obligated to anyone is very unburdening. Like the song lyric goes, "Freedom is just another word for nothing left to lose."

This would take some getting used to.

Ani was working at a 7Eleven store at the time and I would drive her to work every morning before going to my office near by. Our route always took us past both the early morning Hookers standing next to the canal in China Town and a small group of Chinese retirees waiting for the local McDonalds to open at six AM. Their meeting at McDonalds was a regular social event which occurred every day and wouldn't break up until near noon. The Hookers disappeared earlier. I could never understand how there could be much business for a Hooker at that time of day.

While working at this 7Eleven, Ani was witness to an event which doesn't happen often in ones life. A despondent elderly man in a wheelchair incinerated himself with gasoline in the parking lot right next to the store. Ani had a bit of fame when she was interviewed by a TV reporter. There was no connection but at the same store Ani fell and damaged a tendon in her knee which later needed to be corrected with surgery. She was unable to walk for a while so I moved my computer from the office at Intelect into our apartment and no longer had to drive to work.

Our condo was on the third floor of a complex built a mile up the sloop from the beach and I set up my computer next to a window with a view overlooking the ocean below. In the morning, with a cup of coffee and attired only in a lava lava, (a colorful piece of cloth wrapped around the waist) I was ready for work. Doing my job under these conditions was such a small imposition; I occasionally would forget to eat lunch.

Most late afternoons after Ani's knee had improved we would take a long walk down to the beach and then drive along the ocean to the end of the road at the Northern tip of the island. Here, with a cold beer, we would watch the sun sink behind the sea's distant blue horizon. An additional treat could sometimes be had by seeing the "Green Flash." This is a phenomenon which happens just as the sun disc drops out of sight where sea and sky meet and the normal red of its edge changes to green for only a split second before disappearing.

Frequently the sun, now below the horizon, would illuminate the underside of clouds overhead creating the classic sundown picture reproduced thousands of times in tourist brochures. This would be a perfect end to the day.

My life now slipped into a quite routine divided between work and play. On weekends we often rode our motorcycle to the North Shore to watch the surfers and lunch was a pizza with a pitcher of cold beer.

Another one of our frequent activities was perusing the shops in China Town. Here the air was always filled with the delightful odor of food and incense. Ani could spend hours wandering through the shops and I never tired of watching all the short shorts going by.

Speaking of short shorts, I particularly like Waikiki Beach. The atmosphere there is very upbeat because the tourists come expecting to have a good time and they almost always are succeeding. This happy communal attitude creates an air of positive vibes I can feel. Ani would spend time walking through the clothing and jewelry shops while I sat by the sidewalk checking out the passing parade. A Perry Boys Buffet Dinner at dark on the outdoor verandah overlooking the beach was always included.

I must add a disclaimer here and even though it might look like it, I am not on the Hawaiian Tourist Bureau's payroll.

# Chapter Six      Back in California

By the fall of 1989, real-estate values in Hawaii had tripled so we took advantage of this condition and sold our condominium at a substantial profit. In an attempt to improve our housing and with Ani wanting to live life in the fast lane, we decided to buy a house close to my little brother in southern California. This may have been a good decision or not. It's hard to tell what different paths would have presented themselves if other choices had been made. In any event, this was the beginning of the recession of the early nineties and I was, for the first time in my life, unable to find a job. I was always welcome back at Intelect so after trying to find work for several months in California, we returned to Hawaii and moved back on the boat. Ani went back to work for Omar the Tent Man and I resumed where I had left off at Intelect.

After six months, we again returned to California and I tried to find employment but still was not successful. Well it was back to good old dependable Hawaii for the second time. I didn't mind a bit returning to my favorite place in the world but Ani wanted to keep trying for California. After another nine months in Hawaii we were once again in California visiting my brother Richard when Ani found an ad in the paper advertising for a Printed Circuit Designer and insisted I check it out.

You can guess the results. Fatalistically here I was back in Santa Clara where it had all begun so many years earlier. I was now employed at De La Rue Giori, an electronic subsidiary of the largest banknote printing company in Europe.

This company was designing and building a state of the art optical scanner which would be used to detect imperfections in the yard square sheets of money as they came out of the printer. Every individual banknote could be inspected and marked individually if anything like a wart showed up on the Queen's nose.

After two years of development, the design and construction in Santa Clara was finished and I was flown to Milan, Italy to assist in the installation of the electronics on the main assembly being constructed there.

I had the great good fortune to fly business class to Germany on Lufthansa. I am very appreciative to have experienced this kind of luxury one time in my life. This was a thirteen hour flight over the northern part of Canada and Greenland to Frankfort. It was summer time so at these latitudes it stayed daylight for the entire trip. I could see limitless expanses of frozen wetlands in Canada and a crazy quilt pattern of broken ice flows over the northern ocean. I was fully aware of the hostility of the environment just inches away from my face on the other side of the window next to me. If ever I was to be lucky, I wanted it to be now.

Here in Milan, I was housed in a private apartment with all meals included. The day started with a Champaign Breakfast Buffet and ended with a typical Italian Pasta Dinner. The only negative here was all the Television programs available in the evening were broadcast in Italian. Only one station featured a program that could be understood by anyone with normal eyesight. This broadcast was a striptease which followed a strict unwavering routine. A nice looking young lady would be introduced wearing only a bra, panties, garter belt, and long nylon stockings. First, the long nylon stockings were slowly removed one at a time. Next it was the garter belt's turn revealing the panties underneath. Finally with much fanfare, the bra was quickly dropped and just as quickly the camera switched to the announcer introducing the next act. This strict routine was repeated over and over for hours into the night.

Italy seemed to be schizophrenic about sex. A strict Catholic Nation covered boarder to boarder with billboards using topless models selling everything imaginable.

It was here my good luck stepped in again and saved my life. I was working on a system that reportedly was an exact twin to the one we had in California. This however, turned out to be not the case. I had turned off the power on the section I was working on and while changing some components, the power wiring gave met a slight tingling sensation in my hand. I thought at first it was just a nerve impulse but when it persisted I got suspicious. Getting my voltmeter, I tested for power being present and found I had been handling a live 220 volt line with bare hands. If I had touched the frame with one hand while holding the wiring with the other, I would have been electrocuted. The fact that I was wearing rubber soled shoes which insulated me from the ground, also explained why I am still alive. Chock up one more of those uncountable number of times when it's better to be lucky than smart.

Several months after I returned to California, the design work was finally finished and I, like everyone else here at De La Rue Giori, was out of a job.

Now my life story gets really boring.

Still working at a variety of different companies, life became very routine. My typical day would start with going to work around nine in the morning and working until around eight in the evening. The middle of my day usually was as routine. About eleven thirty I would meet my brother Richard for lunch at one of several restaurants we liked or when weather permitted, we would buy sandwiches and picnic in Alviso near where I had built my boat. Being here always reinforced my memories of those earlier days and I found myself wishing I could do it all over again. After eating we would usually go for a long walk on the levee before returning to the office.

The only activity which broke the routine at this time was Richard's Swing Band. He had been playing with a local band in Santa Clara while I was living in Hawaii and shortly after my return to California, he bought the band from its retiring owner. With his wife Lorna as the Vocalist and me as Latin Percussionist, Roady and Sound Engineer, he now had us all involved. We played for Wedding, Birthdays, Holidays and a dozen Dance Clubs every year. I really enjoyed the Latin Percussionist part of my job but, as the Roady, the unpacking and packing of all the equipment left a little to be desired. However as this was another chance to be with my brother, I really didn't mind. After eight years, many jokes were made of the fact that the band had in conjunction with the worlds oldest Roady, a Sound Engineer who was going deaf.

During the years I had been in California, I would have to fly back to Hawaii every spring and renew my boat's mooring permit with the state Harbor Master. This had been a mixed blessing as it gave me an excuse to visit with my old friend Jean-Louis who, during my absence, had the thankless job of minding my boat. The only way we were ever able to repay him was on the occasions when he and his family would go on extended visits to Tahiti, we were forced to house-sit his new luxury home in Aina Haina.

Some sacrifice  Huh?

Anyway, having to put up with the hassle of dealing with the Harbor Master got to be too much of an imposition so I sold my beloved boat.

Finally at the ripe old age of seventy two, I decided to retire and write my memories. It has been one hell of a life. The best part of which was having the extreme good luck of meeting Ani. Even though we only knew each other for eleven days when we married, Ani became the real love of my life and as Lucille, the co-owner of Intelect commented, "It looks like this time it took."

# To Be Continued

# Chapter Seven    A  Time And Place

Hello! I see you have a bit of curiosity about where this all began for me so good luck with the reading.

Small parts of this story are covered in the main narrative so if you find yourself thinking "I already read this" you may be right.

On the year of my birth the population of Holgate was around fifteen hundred souls and at this writing, seventy five years later, the population is still about fifteen hundred souls.

The town has changed but not much.

This is what it looked like for the first eighteen years of my life.

Located in the rural northwestern corner of Ohio, our small town had a distinct country personality. There sure wasn't much here you could put in a Vacation Travel Brochure. Its ambience and atmosphere was defined by the roar and earsplitting whistles of the trains regularly running through its center. The main street, aptly named Railroad Ave. ran next to the tracks for two blocks and terminated at Whilhelm St. on the western end.

These two streets defined the town's entire business district.

At the Eastern end of Railroad Ave. stood The Hotel. Its three story, dark brick, foreboding presents always seemed a little threatening to me when I was young and I always had an uneasy feeling about it. I certainly never once considered venturing inside. The fact that it housed the town's only divorcee probably accounted for much of the fascination we had with this place. A common belief by the post puberty crowd was if one could get a date with her ----- well you know what they say about a divorcee.

Next up the street from The Hotel was the Seed Store. This establishment was apparently never painted. Its gray weathered exterior matched its gray weathered interior and its wood plank floor, polished smooth by farmers' boots and seed bags being dragged about, completed the functional aura of the place.

I remember this store as a small child but not later as a teenager. It either went out of business, fell down, or the owner may have died, but in my typical inattentive young mind, its demise escaped my notice.

Further up the street was my absolute favorite place during my pre-puberty years. Called the Ten Cent Store, this was a general merchandise establishment full of "Gee Gous" and "Jimcracks", our name for things that sit on shelves around the house and have absolutely no function other than to be on display. I rarely made it past the glass enclosed candy counter located in the front center of its single large room. Behind that counter's nose and finger print stained glass, lay a tempting array of penny candies. Here could be found large orange colored peanut shapes and marshmallow pillows with plastic finger rings imbedded in their centers. Small cones with marshmallow ice cream on top lay next to white candy sticks formed to look like lit cigarettes. Also on display were boxes of hollow licorice sticks and my favorite, a Guess What. The latter was a small paper tube closed at both ends which contained several pieces of hard candy and a small toy prize. The name, Guess What, referred to the unknown toy inside. At a time when a minor could go to the movie for thirteen cents, a penny for candy could seem like an important purchase. If my mother had given me fifteen cents, I would buy one box of licorice sticks and a Guess What and still have enough money for the movie.

The corner building at the end of the street was the Red & White grocery store. The proprietor here was a tall angular sort of man who ran his business using an accounting system that was common at that time. As most farmers' income came at irregular intervals and in variable amounts, an accounts book was kept for every customer who would "charge" their purchases and then pay when they were able. As far as I could tell, this system ran completely on trust by both sides. An extra source of income for him was a standup lunch he would provide for the school children. This was the ultimate in simplicity and probably illegal. With a single slice of white bread and a hotdog taken from a pot on a hotplate behind the meat counter, he would provide simple sandwiches to one and all for five cents.

A woman's hat emporium was located just around the corner on Whilhelm St. The fashion of the day dictated all women must have their heads covered in church and I believe this simple fact was only thing that kept this store open. Also a side activity of more interest to the occupants was keeping an eye on the comings and goings of the patrons of the saloon directly across the street. However disappointedly for this bunch of busybodies, most everyone with any illusions of respectability entered the saloon through the back door in the ally.

A place of subdued lighting with an ever present odor of stale beer and tobacco smoke in the air, this saloon was also a good alternative for lunch. The fare here was a slice of roast beef, mashed potatoes with gravy and chocolate milk served in a large beer glass.

The location next to the hat emporium, over the years, had several identities. At one time it was a war surplus store where we occasionally bought clothing which was quite cheap and long lasting. I always wanted a sheepskin lined air force flight jacket but unfortunately, it was considered too expensive. The army field rations were a particular favorite of mine. I am sure the solders using them in the war had few sentimental feelings about them but for some reason I did. The small individual packets of coffee, crackers, and the heat in the can food, seemed somehow to be a treat for me. "Ham and Limas" is still always on my shopping list.

Further up, Whilhelm St. divided into two slightly divergent streets. Here in the junction, a Civil War Naval cannon stood guarding the front of our firehouse. I don't recall ever wondering how a Naval cannon came to be located this far from major body of water. Also I don't recall ever seeing a fire truck so there couldn't have been much of a need for this facility.

Next to the saloon was a clothing store which we also had little need of. All our clothes and shoes were purchased through mail order catalogs like Montgomery Ward and Sears & Roebuck. The only item I have any memory of having been bought in that store was a double breasted suit to be worn by me in Church at my Confirmation. I was sixteen at the time and as the suit size did not conform to my tall slim body, the necessary tailoring of the pants put the pockets nearly together in the back.

I would not own another suit for 20 years.

Back to the walk through, we finally come to the Movie Theater. This building was original designed and built when live stage shows were the only local form of entertainment. The addition of a projection booth in the rear and a movie screen on the back wall of the stage were the only changes made when it was converted into a movie theater. The original dark red wine colored curtains still hung on both sides of the stage and the offset lighting high on the walls illuminated the dirty green scroll designs on the edge of the ceiling.

In those early years the movie ran uninterrupted for two or more showings and we could go in anytime regardless of where in the story it happened to be. We didn't seem to mind if things seemed confusing as we could get it all sorted out the second time around. The movies were our only contact with the world beyond. When I was sitting in that dark fantasy world, cities, mountains, and oceans were all revealed to me. I became a hopeless romantic, always falling in love with the likes of Hedy Lamarr, Paulette Goddard, and Jennifer Jones. I was shown all the different ways a girl's affections could be won and how true love sometimes can be found while dancing. I think it was here I developed my lifelong romantic notion about the way life was supposed to be.

There was nothing like the last building on the street to dispel the dreamy feeling left by the Movie. This was a large metallic looking structure at the end of Railroad Ave. called the Creamery. This building was the processing plant for all the milk and cream collected from the surrounding farms. Strictly utilitarian, not an ounce of romance could be associated with it. There was always a lot of noise and clatter from the two foot high metal milk cans going up the moving ramp from the delivery trucks.

A little distance south of the Creamery was the location of a water filled depression we called the Pond. This was the only exception to the otherwise unrelentingly flat landscape in this part of the state. About the size of a football field and surrounded by small trees, it was a favorite hangout summer and winter. Even though the condition of it's stagnate water did not encourage swimming, it was a popular spot.

Skipping small flat stones on its opaque surface was one popular summer sport and when frozen over in the winter, it provided the only place large enough for ice skating. For relief from the cold, we would build small fires under the trees on its edge and if there was a full moon, this place took on a sort of magical quality matching what we sometimes would see in the Movies.

Another prominent feature in town was the Aerator which treated our city water supply. Coming from a deep well source, the water had a mineral contaminant common in this part of the state. This strong sulfur smelling component had to be removed by constantly pumping the water across a series of horizontal baffles creating a series of small waterfalls. Air flowing through this creation removed the noxious odor. This facility was located next to our city park and when the wind was blowing from the wrong direction, the down wind side became no place for the easily offended. This park was the only recreational facilities available outside our school and it provided only a few swings and a single small merry-go-round. This sturdy devise did provide some welcome entertainment when we would take the smaller kids for a ride. Pushing on the support bars in its center, we could get it spinning so fast it became impossible for the hapless riders to hold on and they would go flying off into the grass. Squealing with laughter, they would immediately clamor back on and do this over and over again.

Finally the only other feature of note in town, the Elevator, was located directly across the railroad tracks from the down town stores. Here all the locally grown grain was delivered, weighted, and stored before being loaded into the waiting railroad cars for shipment to distant markets. Two tall concrete storage silos dominated this location.

The only accident in town that I know of occurred here next to the Elevator where Whilhelm St crossed the railroad tracks. One day on our way home from school in the afternoon, the school bus we were on stalled while crossing and, sitting with its front wheels in the middle of the tracks, refused to start again. It seemed only moments before we saw a train coming from some distance down the track. Our bus driver shouted telling us to get out of the bus immediately. Using both the emergency door in the back and the front door by the driver, everyone got out safely and ran a short distance back down the street. I remember seeing the bus driver desperately trying to push the bus backwards off the tracks but if he had succeeded in moving it a couple of feet, the train would have hit him instead. Finally seeing the futility of his actions, he jumped back out of the way just in time. The images of the bus violently rotating completely around with one of its front wheels rolling down the track next to the still moving train are still vivid in my memory.

This is how I remember this small simple place. Still I do believe I was very fortunate to have been born at that time and in that place. It was a time and place of simplicity and innocence. This was a Tom Sawyer and Huckleberry Fin sort of place without the racial tensions.

All the doors in our house were left unlocked. I don't believe any keys for them ever existed. I can't recall ever being afraid of anything except our bulls and the dark space in the attic above our dining room. This space was accessible through a low door in my sister's upstairs bedroom but there was no way I would have considered exploring it. I was sure some terrible malevolent thing hid in there.

All law enforcement was handled by the county sheriff but if I ever saw him, I was unaware of his identify. Crime simply didn't exist or if it did, there was no reporting of it. The only traffic control in town was one stop sign at the end of Railroad Ave. and as a significant percentage of the traffic in town consisted of farm tractors pulling wagons, no speed limits were needed.

Occasionally small bits of information would sneak into my world like at the outset of World War Two; I remember hearing a report on the radio stating "War clouds are gathering over Europe." I must have been around eight years old and in my mind I took this literally and imagined dark clouds covering the countryside. If there was ever any discussion in my family about politics or world events, I don't recall hearing it. Generally weather was the main topic of interest. Either it was too hot or too cold or there was too much or too little rain. I can appreciate their obsession with the weather as their survival depended on it being favorable.

All our classes in school dealt with general subjects like the three R's with no mention of any current news. Understandably, any education on subjects like sex was totally absent.

There wasn't any sexual education at home either. My mother and father never exhibited any intimacy in our presents and the only demonstrable affection we were exposed to outside of the Movies was when we were young, we would kiss the folks on the cheek goodnight.

So protected from viewing any live intimacy, I recall being embarrassed and titillated one day in school when I spied our teacher kissing the music teacher in our second grade coat room.

We were told the Stork delivered all the children. I was seven years old when my brother Richard was born and my sister Janet and I, discovering a baby in a bassinette in the living room one morning, thought our Aunt Kathryn had come for a visit bringing the latest addition to her family. We had been completely unaware of our mother's pregnancy.

To this day, I cannot create a mental image of anyone I knew at that time, having anything to do with sex. All the adults I knew presented a complete asexual form to us.

Living among animals on the farm, I had seen many examples of sexual activity but I always thought they were only playing or fighting. We under aged received all our information from each other. For example, one day while playing under the civil war cannon in town, I received my initial detailed sexual education from a friend two years my junior. He outlined for me the basic mechanics of the sex act and later at home, I ask my mother for verification of this new revelation. After she filled in some of the missing details, my response was "Why would anyone want to do something like that?" She completed my education with the question, "Do you know what passion is?" I certainly must have been pre-puberty because I was still mystified.

Slowly though, I began to see the light. So that is what this masturbation thing was all about. I had always liked girls with cute faces but now my interest had shifted farther south.

I must have been radiating something at about the time of my puberty because our neighbor's older daughter Marie, at age sixteen had formed a girlish crush on me. As I, at fourteen, was taller than she was, our age difference didn't seem to matter. It was at the hands of this sweet, wonderful, charming, giving, generous, delightful, young lady that I experienced my first intimate mouth kiss. I was leaving the barn carrying a bucket of milk in each hand when she took advantage of my defenseless position and planted one on me. I decided then and there, I wanted a lot more of this. I think her parents got wind of the situation when they found us lying in the hay stack with my head in her lap. It was all very innocent, but they nipped it in the bud.

The actors in the movies were my only romantic role models. The stories at that time also depicted an innocence that even I didn't buy. When a husband seemed surprised to find his wife was going to have a baby, my reaction was "How can he be surprised when he was there when she got pregnant." Maybe, because in the movies at that time, all married couples slept in separate beds, some surprise by the husband can be expected.

Consistent with our isolated way of life was the fact that the inhabitants of our small community were all white, Christian, and mostly of German descent. Lacking any of the many minorities common in large cities, we were not advantaged with a lot of preconceived ideas about how to regard people who were different from us. But like all societies, we did have some social tensions. There were the Protestants on one hand and the Catholics on the other. Additionally the High Germans looked down with distain on the Low Germans whose feelings were apparently mutual. I remember hearing Maw muttering at the sight of our (Low German) neighbor passing on the road "Stiff headed low Dutch. Too good to look in and wave." No one ever explained what High German and Low German meant except I believe it had to do with what part of Europe your ancestors came from. Then of course there were those who frequented the local saloon and those who did not. And finally; there were those who bathed regularly and those who apparently did not. The latter were referred to as "Trash", a handy term for anyone of a perceived lower class. Many of the individuals here belonged to more than one of the above groups.

The only contact we had with strangers happened during the Great Depression of the thirties when occasionally a vagrant man walking the railroad tracks past our farm would stop and ask for food. My mother would always manage to find something for them which they generally accepted with gratitude but on one occasion, the recipient of her generosity committed an unforgivable offence when he removed and discarded the fat from the ham sandwich she had made. I guess her belief that "Beggars can't be choosers" is what bothered her the most. We referred to these people as "Bums." Uniformly unwashed and drably clothed, they appeared somewhat menacing and I was always a little apprehensive when one would show up on our doorstep.

Looking back, I realize many of the inhabitants of this place may have been unique to say the least. One family up the road consisted of a brother and sister who lived most of their life together. My folks would always complain about the difficulty visiting with them because they both would always talk at the same time making any listener having to choose which one to listen to and which one to ignore. Only after the sister died late in life, did the brother find a wife.

I had two great uncles who, while remaining unmarried, lived their entire lives together and died of old age within months of each other.

Also two of my school mates, apparently being the only ones left single in their age group, finally married in their forties.

I had a distant cousin who was talked about because wore long winter underwear all year round.

# Chapter Eight    I Yam What I Yam

Let me begin here by introducing you to my Family.

By way of identification, we all called my paternal grandfather and paternal grandmother Paw and Maw. Beside myself, there is my sister Janet one year behind me, my brother Richard seven years younger and my baby brother Curtis who came along an additional eight years later. All the brothers had the good sense to get an education and make it out of the crazy early part of early adulthood by being in the military. My sister chose to be married forever and make as many babies as possible.

My Father was an only child who was dealt a hand by Fate which he was not able to fully except or reject. He was a very intelligent sensitive man who I believe would have been much more fulfilled and happier in a challenging technical occupation but as the soul responsible caretaker for his mother and invalid father, he opted to stay on the farm where he was born. If my Father ever had any hope of leaving the farm, his fate was sealed when Paw died. I was seven years old at the time and the only memory I have of him is his teaching me to make a rhythm with my hands on my knees and promising to let me fire our 22 caliber rifle when I was older.

I have no way of knowing if my family was very different than any other who lived and worked on a farm at that time. None of us children were ever included in any adult conversations. Discussions about lifestyles and careers were totally lacking. We were talked to only to receive instructions on behavior. My mother had a great sense of humor but if my father ever thought anything was funny, he kept it well hidden. My only interaction with him was connected with work on the farm. I don't think he had any interest in sports of any kind and he certainly didn't play any games with me. Forty years after his death, while reading some letters he had sent to my mother before they were married, I found he had a wit and humor he had never revealed to me.

My family was Protestant Christian but I wasn't. They tried to make me one but they failed. My father was not a religious fanatic but as financial secretary and custodian of our church for many years, he was quite active in its business. This meant we were the first to arrive at church on Sunday mornings to prepare for services and in the winter, going to light its coal furnace, our car tracts were always the first in the morning snow. After collecting the monitory offering to be counted and later deposited in the bank, we were the last to leave at the end of services. Having these responsible positions made it necessary for us to attend services every Sunday without exception. There was always something to do year round. Mowing the grass around the Church and adjoining Grave Yard in the spring and summer yielded to raking and burning leaves in the fall. Shoveling snow off the sidewalks in winter always provided a handy way to keep warm.

One activity I found particularly unpleasant was our required presents at all the funerals held in Church. As a result, the odor of a large mixture of flowers still reminds me of death.

From the beginning, I dutifully attended Sunday school and later when I was sixteen, the obligatory Confirmation classes. The latter of these were designed to prepare the children for full church membership and at there completion, a well rehearsed oral test was given in front of the full congregation. Who did they think they were fooling?

I had been going through the motions of believing all I was taught but in reality, I was only faking it. I went through the correct motions and bowed my head during prayers but my mind was always elsewhere. I originally didn't have a choice but finally at sixteen, I exercised a little independence. I still could not avoid having to go to the Church on Sundays but now I managed to remain outside during the services. I would look through the parking lot for a car with a radio and lounge there listening to music until the service was over. Only then would I go inside to help with our custodial duties. For some reason, this religion thing just didn't make any sense to me and I just wasn't buying it.

But why was I not buying it? Rarely does anyone question

the source of their beliefs. Simple observation of most of the rest of the world indicated an overwhelming willingness of the masses to believe what their parents believed. A suicide bomber about to blow himself up cannot have any doubts about the correctness of his beliefs. The thought that he might not be doing this if his father, and therefore he, had belonged to a different religion can not have enter his mind. This obviously is why we don't see many Atheist suicide bombers.

After all, who could believe time, space, and billions of galaxies were created just to impress humans who originally had no way of knowing they existed. Did you ever think maybe it could be creation on demand? There is no object in creating stuff that couldn't be seen by anyone. I can see it now, God muttering to himself, "Well there they go building a bigger telescope so I better create something for them to look at." Can you imagine how exciting it got for him when man started investigating the world of particle physics? Trying to keep up must have taken his breath away.

Have you ever thought that there is as much eternity behind us as there is in front? Just think what a waste of eternity it was when it went by and we missed it. One can only wonder how God managed alone without human companionship for all of that time in the past.

When did this totally illogical God myth get started and why does it persist so universally?

I have a theory.

Once upon a time in the dim beginnings of mans mental evolution there had to have been, at some point, the first glimmer of the mental activity we call imagination. Perhaps cowering in the dark in fear of all their known dangers, the concept of an unknown danger emerged. The ability to form a mental image of a force beyond that which could be seen or touched would have been the first emergence into the world of imagination. They obviously could see and feel things like fire or lightening but it would take imagination to form a spiritual component associated with it. You can not see or feel a spirit. You can only imagine it. This must have been the origin of the superstitions and myths which slowly grew into the cohesive and recognizable religious forms we see today.

The origin of the belief that we have a soul must be the result of our survival instinct combined with our ego. All living things have a survival instinct proved by the fact they survived. But you will notice only living things with egos believe they have a soul.

Why it's as plain as the nose on your face that we are so important we simply could not just cease to exist when we die. So therefore there has to be a life after death. All religions agree on that one point. This view of an afterlife extends from ancestor worship and reincarnation in animal or human form to an eternity of bliss with some mystical god.

The histories of all religions follow a similar path. Originally man's concerns with gods were limited to pacifying them hoping for rewards in the present.

When it became obvious that appeasing the Gods was not reliably successful, another idea related to getting your rewards in an afterlife became more popular as it couldn't be disproved.

There is little to be gained from long detailed discussions arguing the merits and validity of the many different religions except to say they all have the same origin.

If God created Man in His Image or Man created God in his image, the result would be the same.

Having been indoctrinated into only the Christian Religion, I can not speak as an authority on any other but they can't be any sillier than Christianity. The center post of Christianity is the death of Jesus. How can you kill a God? If Jesus was a God in human form who could perform miracles, raise the dead, cure the blind and heal the lame, he certainly could have done what any ordinary Indian Fakir or Hypnotized Californian can do. Ignore Pain!!!

The second most farfetched idea is that by killing God, (He was only dead for three days by the way) all of humanities transgressions will be forgiven. This sacrifice might have been the ultimate enactment of the Traditional Jewish sacrificial Lamb. In fact Christ is referred to as The Lamb Of God

And another very lucky thing happened for Christians. Jesus was a Jew who lived at a time when reportedly, the instrument of execution was a simple wooden cross. What if he had been a Frenchman living during the latter part of 18th Century. Would we see church steeples adorned with large illuminated Guillotines? Would little girls going to Sunday school be wearing small gold Guillotines on gold threads around their necks? And would the Priests in Vampire Movies ward off the evil one with a foot long light radiating Guillotine? Just imagine every crucifix you've ever seen being replaced with a corpse lying on a Guillotine with his head in a basket. Also he probably wouldn't have been a Jew so his ministry would have been devoid of the long rich mono-theistic history it actually has. Imagine what Christianity would be like if everything in the Old Testament was removed.

Now let us take a look at what is promised in our afterlife. The early Egyptians had a more realistic idea I think. They included in the Tomb with the departed, all the earthly pleasures available for later use in the afterlife.

Now here's an interesting idea.

A designer Heaven. What if everyone was given the option of designing their own individual Heaven? Now wouldn't that be a lot more fair and democratic than to have to spend eternity in a "one size fits all" offering.

The diversity available to us during our earthly sojourn doesn't seem sufficient to completely satisfy us for the short time we have here and now we propose to look forward with great expectation to an eternity of exact sameness. Some have found this condition already. It's called a permanent drug induced high.

There is ample proof that we can get used to anything pleasurable and only if occasionally deprived do we appreciate advantage. I am reminded of the story of the man who died and thought he was in heaven because his every desire was immediately fulfilled. Ultimately, extremely bored and unfulfilled by the lack of any challenges, he asked to be transferred to "the other place". Only then to be told, "You are in the other place"

# Chapter Nine     School And Me

I have to apologies here for the next part of the story. I didn't like school at all so I don't think this part of my life is very interesting but in an attempt to be complete, it is included.

I began attending our local school at six years of age and over the years developed an intense dislike for the institution and everything connected with it.

Every school day we were picked up and returned home in a school bus which followed a long, winding route up and down the country roads to access all the families with children. This, plus the normal school period made a nine-hour school day. Time that I thought much better spent in other activities.

Our school was a single two story brick structure which contained the entire educational system for the Township.

Occupying a significant part of this building was the Gymnasium/Assembly Hall. Here a basketball court dominated the center with a drama stage on one side and a sloping seating section on the other. During basketball games, additional seating was provided by erecting wooden bleachers on the stage and during stage activities temporary seating was added on the basketball court. The entire school also used the basketball court for all indoor extra curricular activity. The lower grade teachers used it for games like Drop the Handkerchief, Farmer in the Dell, and Ring around the Rosy. Large thick floor mats were stored under the stage and were available when needed for tumbling and other exercises. We had no equipment or programs for any sports other than Basketball and Baseball. I did not participate in either of these as I had no particular talent or interest but even if I did, needing to be at home to do my daily chores on the farm precluded staying after school for practice.

My interest never was in organized sports but rather in gymnastics. I practiced riding my bicycle while sitting backwards on the handlebars and peddling from that position. Walking on my hands, cartwheels, forward flips and barrel walking were also well rehearsed in our barnyard.

All outdoor recreational facilities including the Baseball

Diamond were located in a large open area behind the school. A concrete bleacher section with its protective wire mesh barrier facing the first base line was the only seating provided. We used the angular framework supporting this barrier as monkey bars and, with legs wrapped tightly around, would overhand all the way to its twenty five foot high summit. If we had fallen on the concrete risers below we might have been fatally injured.

Located to the side of the bleachers were several chain link swings which were in constant use. One game we played on these swings was pumping as high as we could and then at a point which yielded the most height and speed, bail out in an effort to land as far out as we could manage. We were never injured because the landing zone here was a small mound of fine gravel which buffered our landing somewhat. This was a contest with oneself and no distance record was ever recorded.

In those days there didn't seem to be any concern by the establishment for the safety of the children. The theory that we were all rugged individualists who could take care of ourselves was probably good psychological training.

During World War Two the area by the swings was used as a depository for scrap rubber and metal collected for recycling and reuse. At that time all of us were engaged in collecting and this pile grew to an enormous size. I don't know if any of it actually was recycled but it made us feel we were doing something for the war effort.

Well that was it in the recreational department. Basketball and Baseball were the only two organized sports available but there were in addition, two unsanctioned open field games played at lunch time. One was a sort of soccer game played in the Baseball Diamond outfield. Using a football instead of a soccer ball, the rules were quite simple. Any number of players could participate and only kicking the ball and the chins of whoever was in the way, were permitted. Due to the erratic movement of the football, very little kicking technique could be developed. At the start of the game, the ball was placed roughly in the middle of the field and the two opposing mobs would back off and then on a signal, charge!

I no longer remember the method used for dividing the mob into two more or less equal sizes but somehow they were. Sometimes a more aggressive people on one side would compensate for slightly larger numbers on the opposing side. Unlike hockey and soccer, the goal here was simply kicking the ball out of the playing field. Not much science but great fun none the less.

The second game was sort of a king of the hill contest. Each participating team consisted of one boy carrying another boy piggy back. The sole object was to unhorse the rider of your opponent in any way possible. Generally, one would attempt to pull the rider off his mount so the winner in this case would be determined by the strength and determination of the horse. Many other strategies like ramming, tripping and outrunning your opponent were also common. This mayhem would continue until only one duo was left intact. As I was one of the bigger boys, I always had the honor of being the horse and never the rider. My good friend Danny was always sought as the horse as he was built with a slightly protruding rear which made a more secure perch for a rider. I always thought this game had potential for inclusion in the Olympics.

One tragic outcome of these rough house games was my cousin Vernon received an accidental kick in the temple while lying on the ground. Suffering a brain hemorrhage, he died two weeks later. That family had more than its share of misfortune. Vernon's older brother Howard, lost his vision on one side when he was hit in the eye by a green plum thrown in jest.

During the time I was incarcerated in this institution, the average class mustered no more than twenty five souls. I was kept with the same core group of inmates for the entire length of my sentence.

In the lower grades there existed a rough division in the social standing of the individuals which separated the teachers pets (all girls) from the rest of us. Then later in High school, there was a definite social stratification among the girls which I was never able to understand. It didn't seem to be based on any one thing like who was the prettiest or whose father was the most affluent. The snootiest of the bunch did exhibit an open distain for us country boys. I suppose the image of a kid whose entire wardrobe consisted of bibbed overalls is hard to forget.

It seems really strange to me now but I don't recall having a single verbal exchange with any of these girls during the entire time I was forced to associate with them.

Viewed from my present perspective, I feel really sorry for one girl who, through no fault of her own, had the misfortune of being born into one of the families we classified as Trash. This classification was apparently based on her family's inability to buy soap. I now really admire her for presenting a brave front and an air of normalsy to what I can only imagine was an inexcusably cruel situation. If only I had then the "in your face" attitude I would develop latter in life, I would have delighted in giving the bird to the rest of the snobs by befriending her. I am glad now I didn't because it would have been a kind gesture for all the wrong reasons and could have done more harm than good.

One other sad situation here was a family who had two severely retarded children. The older girl and her brother were so handicapped they were unable to even communicate in any meaningful way. Their parents sent them to school every day thinking it would be better if they could interact with other children but I am not sure this was a good idea. They obviously needed special schooling.

There was less differentiation among the boys. What existed was based on their athletic interest. Jocks were always more popular with the girls. I think the impressions made in the early years followed one all through school.

From as far back as I can remember my two best friends were Daniel Gray and Donald Tadson. Dan's father was the Shop teacher in High School and Don's father worked in a factory in Toledo and was home in Holgate only on weekends. Even though we would frequently stay overnight at each others houses, we rarely had any interaction with our fathers. It seems fathers are to be avoided whenever possible as we seemed to feel we were doing something wrong all the time. Truth be known, we probably were.

Mothers on the other hand were another matter. These people were the much appreciated purveyors of food and smiles.

Another friend who I would trade overnight visits with was Dick Knapp. He was not very popular in school and I must have felt a little sorry for him for I would choose his side in tussles with the other boys. My altruistic motives might have been suspect because his sister Diane was the cutest and most darling girl I knew. One year younger than me, she was the object of all my spin the bottle fantasies.

Remembering First Grade in school leaves me with only a few images. The ABCs were displayed in longhand and print along the top of the wall all the way around the room. My teachers name was Miss Rethmal. Like all our teachers at that time, she was unmarried and apparently on her way to making this a permanent condition. Quite tall and thin, she resembled a hard bitten character from a Norman Rockwell painting. One day I had some sort of a minor altercation in line with another boy my age and as a result, we both were sentenced to a paddling. At that time a paddling was a literal threat as a large heavy wooden paddle was the instrument of choice. I sure didn't think our little tussle warranted this type of corporal punishment. We were given the choice of receiving it immediately or waiting until the end of the day. We chose waiting thinking she might forget all about it. We were wrong and later were subjected to this humiliation in front of the class. I had received a switching from my father quite a few times so a little paddling didn't amount to much but it was the humiliation and later teasing I received that hurt the most. These kinds of "spare the rod, spoil the child" treatments were common and accepted universally at that time. There were strict laws of behavior in school which were enforced by the frustrated, unmarried, old maid teachers especially screened for the job. No chewing gum, no talking in class without permission and no running in the halls were but a few of many restrictions.

One of my teachers in junior high had taught my father. She had a strange way of counting on her fingers which kept the entire class in a constant state. Making a point, she would pull one finger at a time back until it looked like it would break. No one ever listened to what she was saying, only waited for that finger to break or at least slip and hit her in the face. I don't recall knowing for sure but it looks to me now as though one of the requirements for employment as a teacher was they be and remain unmarried. If that was true then it explains a lot about their attitudes.

I can't remember if we started reading in the First or Second grade but whenever it was, we were taught to read using the Phonic method. I remember reciting all the different sounds like hog, bog, log, fog, and hit, bit, sit fit. I had no problem in mastering this art but was and I am a complete failure at spelling. Whenever I was forced into any kind of spelling bee, I would immediately miss-spell the first word I was given so I could get it over with and sit down. I knew if the word had more than two letters in it, I would get it wrong.

Another component in our education in the Second Grade was the Rhythm Band. This consisted of beating out rhythms using one of several different instruments. One was a type of clapper resembling a large wooden spoon with two round ends which when moved briskly would strike the center piece making a sharp clapping sound; hence the name clapper. Another instrument was no more than two pencil size wooden sticks which were merely tapped together to keep time with the group. I was always disappointed to not get to play the clappers but was instead given a pair of the more plentiful sticks. There must have been even in the second grade a type of discrimination. Finally there were metal triangles to add a bit of music to the din. I always thought people were born with a sense of rhythm but maybe not. Why else would they teach it to us in the lower grades? I have no way of knowing if my practice on the sticks conditioned me for much later in life when I would be playing Latin percussion in my brother's swing band.

I started disliking going to school at about the Fourth Grade and I became a very uncooperative student. I did get a short reprieve from this duty when I contracted Scarlet Fever. At that time, six weeks of quarantine was required and I was banished to our only downstairs bedroom. It must have been late in the school year because it was warm enough for me to have the bedroom window open. To break the boredom, I had managed to attach a length of string to the wooden handle of an ice pick and while leaning out the window, I could throw it and attempt to make it land pointed end down and stick in the yard. The only other diversion I had was my radio. Beside all the afternoon children programs my favorites were the evening Big Band broadcasts from the Ballrooms of the Hotels in New York. I still remember many of the songs I learned from those broadcasts. Luckily, my school lessons were somehow made available to me and I managed to pass to the next Grade at the end of the year.

From this point on, I barely managed to squeak through without "failing." At years end, it was always with great dread that I would examine my final report card to see if I had made it to the next Grade. I really have no idea why I disliked school so much.

Later in Junior High I really rebelled. As though a nine hour school day wasn't enough, now I was expected to donate additional time in the evening doing homework. I simply could not force myself to do it. I thought school was supposed to be a place where one went to learn and have knowledge provided by a teacher. The operative word here is "Teacher." The reality of the situation seemed to me to be one where I was required to teach myself at home with homework and the teacher's responsibility was to determine in class the next day, how well I had done on my own the night before. The inevitable result was, if I was called on early in the period, I naturally was unable to provide much information. However at the end of the class discussion each day, I knew as much as I would if I had done the homework. This resulted in my receiving failing grades in daily work and passing grades on all my examinations. The constant anxiety of not being prepared bore heavily on me but not enough to make me change my ways. I could have done some of my homework during periods in the day called Study Hall. I was confined to our home room at these times but instead of studying, I would read the Encyclopedia Britannica or the Encyclopedia Americana. I did well in Biology; one subject which had very little home work and was of some interest to me. I still remember the names of all the bones and muscles in the human body.

In those days a sixteen year old could be excused from

further schooling if he was needed to work on the farm and when as I reached that age, I talked my father into relieving me of this unhappy duty. This didn't take much persuasion as the word Collage simply did not exist in my parents' vocabulary. What an exhilarated feeling this was for me to no longer have to get up every morning and report to that unforgiving institution. Now I thought my life would be one long summer.

Ah the delusions of youth.

# Chapter Ten    On and Off the Farm

Howdy there Partner. Welcome to Hicksville. This section of the story relates to how we lived and generally what our life was like on our small farm. The layout of our home place consisted of a three bedroom two story house with a basement accompanied by a detached garage/workshop. A large hip-roofed barn, a smaller corn and grain storage barn and a machine storage shed completed the plan.

The Nickel Plate Railroad, exiting town in a North-East direction cut off a small corner of our farm. Strangely, I never considered living close to the railroad tracks a particularly negative part of life. The number of trains passing here was no more than one or two a day and besides, the tracks provided a handy two mile shortcut through the farm fields when we were walking to town. The most frustrating part of walking on railroad tracks is the spacing of the wooden cross ties which are positioned at half stride intervals. Stepping on every one requires baby steps and stepping on every other one requires giant steps. Small wonder we would frequently do a tight rope balancing act by simply walking on the rails.

A small amount of coal dropping from the train's coal-cars could always be found along these tracks and as anything could be made into a game, my sister Janet and I would make this a treasure hunt. Walking along the tracks carrying a bucket, we would collect what we could and I was always pleased if we had found what I considered a significant amount. I felt this was helping to support the family in a small way.

In summer the sloping sides of the tracts also provided a steady supply of wild strawberries. Though very small, they contained much more flavor than the much larger domestic variety and every year, Maw would make an ample supply of strawberry preserves from this wild source. Another plant that grew unattended along the roadside was the elderberry bush. The berries from this source were also made into preserves and in addition, Paw would sometimes use them to make elderberry wine. In addition to what grew wild, we ate for the most part only what the farm provided. Peaches, pears, corn, pickles, and peas were preserved in season and with large crocks of curing sauerkraut, stored in the basement. Every year in the fall we would butcher a pig and preserve the meat in a variety of ways. Initially all the excess fat would be trimmed from the meat and put into a large iron kettle hung over a wood fire and cooked to render out all the lard, leaving a tasty crisp item we called cracklings. Hams and bacon were sugar cured and after being cleaned, the pig's intestines were stuffed with ground meat to make sausages. These were then cooked, placed in glass jars and sealed by floating a layer of lard on top. We also preserved by canning, another type of pork meat we called Prettles. The official name of this recipe is Goetta and I have no idea why we called it Prettles. Resembling cold oatmeal, this was a mixture of pork meat, and pin oats flavored with spices which was later prepared by slicing and frying to a golden brown. Another common dish was ground corn meal, cooked like a hot serial and when cold, could be sliced and fried. This was then served with sweet syrup or honey. Apple Strudel sprinkled with sugar and covered with warm milk was occasionally served as a main dish at supper time. Eggs were fried crispy brown "one size fits all" and served on a single large platter. Fried chicken was usually reserved for special occasions. We raised them, not to eat, but for their eggs. Needless to say, we didn't support many roosters. One of my favorite dishes was a wilt salad made with dandelion leaves, bacon bits, and cold boiled potatoes in a milk salad dressing. When in season, sweet corn on the cob would frequently serve as the only item on the menu. We had one way of eating which I found to be unique. Any vegetables such as sauerkraut, peas, corn, or string beans were used, not as a side dish but as gravy on mashed potatoes.

My father was a meat and potatoes man who didn't care to experiment much in the food department. If Mom would ask Maw for a suggestion on what to make for dinner, Maw would automatically reply, "I'll peel the potatoes." It was a given, potatoes would be on the menu. Once in an attempt to create a little variety in our usual menu, Mom made chili and when asked for an opinion, my father replied, "You would have to be a

Mexican to eat it every day."

Fish was another very infrequently seen item on our table. The only fish I can remember having was a local variety called Sheepshead. These fish contained millions of very fine bones, making them difficult to eat. I didn't think the effort needed to avoid the bones was worth the reward.

For the first eight years of my life, we lived without electricity or indoor plumbing. A small room off of the dining room called the washroom contained a hand pump connected to a cistern where run off rain water from the roof was stored. This water was used only for washing and not for consumption. A water bucket with a communal dipper sat on the kitchen counter and provided water for cooking and drinking. This bucket was filled by hand pumping from our deep well in the yard and when my sister Janet or I were assigned to this task, we were so small we would have to first hang on the pump handle to pull it down half way before we could finish by pushing at the bottom of the stroke. I remember doing a lot of pumping to supply enough water for all our animals. I do not know why we had two sources for water but I know the rain water in the cistern, being free from minerals, made much better use of the homemade soap we used at that time. This soap was a concoction of lard and lye which smelled bad but worked fairly well.

Our bathroom facility for bathing was warm water in a galvanized laundry tub sitting next to the coal stove in the dining room. I don't know why this room was called the dining room. It might have been used that way at one time but during my entire life we always ate in the kitchen. Because the only source of heat in the house was located here, this room was instead, used as a utility space for a variety of activities depending on the need and season.

Our toilet facilities were basic country design. A wooden box with a galvanized bucket inside was located in the washroom and a two-hole outhouse behind the garage did duty in good weather.

I never understood why all of the outhouses in our part of the country were built with two holes. Janet and I would frequently use ours at the same time and we each had our reserved hole.

Being alone and bored in there one day, I entertained myself by pounding a circle of dimpled impressions around the seat on her side and later in retaliation, she vindictively rendered my side rough and splintered. I, being the older and stronger, now made her switch sides when we were joint occupants and she thereafter was forced to sit on the splintered side. Strangely, my folks never mentioned even noticing the results of our outhouse wars.

Janet and I must have been a real trial for our parents at times. One hot summer day we had decided to cool off by dumping water on each other while perched on our front porch roof.. Our father being wakened from his nap took exception to this noisy activity and chased us around the house swinging a small rope as a whip. As it was required to howl at the top of your lungs when being punished, we obliged. My cries were genuine but Janet was faking her discomfort. Upon rounding the corner of the house out of sight of our father, she broke into laughter as the wet dress she was wearing hung loosely at her sides and absorbed the impact of the rope without touching her body. I got my revenge another time when we were playing horse. We had draped a small blanket over our bent over bodies with me in front and her following blindly behind. I could see where we were going of course and I trotted directly at a tree in our front yard. At the last second I stepped aside and Janet trotted, head down, straight into the tree. Our father observed this event also and while holding a handful of my shirtfront, shook his fist in my face with the exclamation "I don't know what I'm going to do with you." I guess he decided what to do as he punched me in the nose. It wasn't a hard punch but it did bring tears to my eyes.

After going to bed we would frequently play word games like "I'm hiding in a place that begins with (insert alpha character here)." This game was a precursor to the later popular radio and TV show, Twenty Questions. For years our nightly routine after going to bed was getting scolded by our mother and told to shut up and go to sleep. We would then continue talking but in lower tones. When we heard rapid footsteps approaching the staircase below, we knew the game was up and fell silent but we never gave up easily. I never knew why our parents were so upset by our talking. Maybe it was because they had such a difficult time getting us out of bed every morning.

With the arrival of electricity in 1939, things greatly improved. The washroom was converted into a real bathroom with a toilet and shower. Our deep well was electrified and fresh water under pressure was piped to the house and barn. We were lucky to have sweet water from our well as our closes neighbor only a quarter of a mile distant, had a deep well that delivered strong sulfur smelling water with small black flecks of mineral deposits floating in it. The only negative result of using our farm water supply was its high florin content stained all our teeth with a mottled brown pattern. Reportedly it also makes teeth immune to decay but in our family there was mixed results along this line. Many times I have been asked by children who have no sense of protocol, "Why don't you brush your teeth?"

A source of indoor entertainment made possible by the availability of electricity was the radio. At lunch time, Mom and Maw would listen to Soaps like Pepper Young's Family, The Guiding Light, and Maw Perkins. In the afternoon after school we would listen to Jack Armstrong the All American Boy, Superman and Terry and the Pirates. I can remember lying on the floor in the evening and listening to radio dramas like The Shadow, I Love a Mystery and The Inner Sanctum Mysteries. Using words alone, these radio dramas had the ability to create vivid images in my mind and these images still remain with me to this day..

The ability to see with your mind instead of your eyes is a form of imagination we all have and even though I have no proof that imagination can be made stronger with exercise, I do believe the juvenal activity of "Make Believe" is good preparation for inventiveness in adulthood. When I was young, my environment demanded a great deal of imagination to fill in the missing details my real world lacked. Make believe was involved in all my games. A blanket draped across two kitchen chairs magically became a tent in the woods. Sitting between the legs of a kitchen chair tipped onto its face was enough of a beginning to pretend I was a fighter pilot on patrol over enemy lines. Astride an old broom with the bristle end up to simulate a horse's head, I galloped across the yard slapping my rear with my free hand to make my "horse" go faster. All my toys were made of the simplest materials. My airplanes consisted of two wooden slats nailed together in the form of a cross and could be made to fly by spinning them around on the end of a length of string nailed to the end of the wing. The fact that they would fly forwards, backwards and upside down didn't matter when imagination is strong enough. We built play-houses which were nothing more than boards laid on the ground to define the walls and boards placed across cement blocks for furniture. A few chipped plates and discarded bottles completed the furnishings.

My little Red Flyer wagon was in my mind, a real race car. While kneeling on it with one leg and using my other leg for propulsion, I would repeatedly race down our side walk toward our gravel driveway and arriving at the end, turn sharply scattering stones in every direction. Never tiring, I would repeat this little race over and over again.

The wood-lot on the back corner of our farm was another place where my imagination was useful. In my early teens, I had a romantic notion of what it would be like to be a mountain man and beaver trapper. Most of the books I read at the time were about the exploits of these men and I imagined I would be one someday. I built lean-tos and made small campfires which luckily didn't burn down the woods. I made my own leather moccasins and braided a short rope from strips of leather cut from an old discarded leather jacket. I would sit in my shelter by the fire and pretend I was living like one of the characters in my books. Imagination was hard at work here also.

Then the first warm days of spring would signal the time had come for removing shoes and rebuilding softened feet for the rigors of summer ahead. Running with bare feet through the young grass for the first time was always a delightful experience. Later our yards would fill with bright yellow Dandelion blossoms and now, accidentally stepping on one of the hundreds of Honey Bees swarming in for nectar became a constant threat.

Another consequence of not wearing shoes was inevitably stepping on one or two rusty nails every summer. This was an ever present hazard when searching through our board pile looking for material for whatever project we were working on.

One time as I was leaving the house, I stepped on a sewing needle secreted in a small rug lying on the steps. I only felt a slight prick and when I examined it, all I could see was the eye of the needle still protruding from the skin on the bottom of my foot. Being unable to extract it with my fingers, I hobbled out to the garage and there using a pair of pliers, I was able to pull it free. Strangely, a single smooth spurt of blood the same diameter as the needle exited my wound and that was it. I went on about my business without another thought.

We were now on furlough from school for three months and the stifling heat of summer was still to come. This was the time for watching the tadpoles mature in the ditch that ran along the road by our house. This ditch normally had no water in it but for a short time in the spring the rains would provide enough water for the frogs to get the next generation started. Also this was the time for preparing the garden for planting. The cool moist upturned earth under our feet felt extra nice as we pulled the hoe along making a shallow trench where lettuce, carrots, onions, cabbage and radishes would be planted. This kitchen garden would be replanted throughout the summer as one crop was consumed and another started.

As summer came on and the weather grew warmer, the most uncomfortable part of living here in Ohio was, with the heat, the high humidity and lack of a breeze made sleeping at night difficult. Some times to escape these stifling conditions, I would climb out our bedroom window and lay on the cool tin porch roof. Looking back, I don't understand why we didn't have at least a small electric fan to stir the air around our bed.

Another routine summer activity was wading in the creek and trying to catch the small inch long silver minnows which always seemed to be present. I think these were mature fish as they never seemed to get any bigger. Luckily they were in no danger of extinction for their ability to evade capture was many times greater than our snatching prowess. Sharing the creek bottom with the minnows were many small brown crayfish. These creatures sometimes called crabs, crawdads, and crawfish were even more difficult to catch. We only pursued them for sport and not for food. The idea of eating these spiny creatures never entered my mind. I have often thought that if crabs or lobsters lived on land rather than in the sea they would have been viewed as very large insects and would never been considered edible.

Miraculously these creatures manage to survive somehow under the frozen surface of the creek in winter. The winters here in Ohio were a mixture of very pleasant and unpleasant weather. Occasionally the weather would set up a condition called sleet. When this happened, rain would freeze on everything. Tree limbs, fence wires, grass blades, and electrical wires would be incased in over a quarter of an inch of ice. By contrast there was always something magic about a day without wind when big fluffy snow flakes would drift slowly down and cover everything with a thick white blanket. This much snow would absorb a lot of sound giving the entire countryside a hushed and calm feeling.

At other times, the wind would create snowdrifts across the roads so the school bus couldn't make it through. These times were always a welcome break in the school routine. Snowdrifts were nature's gift to snow cave builders like Janet and I. We would hollow out large enough cavities in the snow to hold the two of us and just huddle inside and pretend to be Eskimos. Our barnyard would routinely be filled with snow forts. These were built by rolling large snowballs into a continuous wall behind which we would hide and throw snow missiles at each other. Eventually the cold would drive us indoors to the heat of our coal-burning stove. That stove was the center of all activity during the winter. Sitting just inside the front door it was the sole source of heat for our entire two-story house. Our upper floor contained two bedrooms accessed by a steep enclosed stairway with a closed door at its base. Only the larger of the two upstairs bedrooms received a little heat through a small grating in the floor. This was of course Janet's room. My little brother Richard and I shared the smaller totally unheated room which at times would have snow accumulate on the windowsill next to our bed. Except for the area immediately around the coal stove, the rest of the house didn't get much heat either.

A typical routine in getting ready for bed in winter was holding a blanket up close to the stove to let it get as hot as you could without setting it on fire and then, after wrapping the warmed blanket tightly around your body, run at top speed for the bedroom and jump in under the cold blankets. Doing this, one always initially lay in a fetal position but after awhile when this position became too uncomfortable, one needed to straighten out. The shock of the body encroaching into the unheated areas of the bed made this a choice of last resort.

One good aspect of winter was Christmas. This was one time of the year I enjoyed very much when we were young. There would always be a service on Christmas Eve and a part of that event was the passing out of bags of candy to all the families with children. Store bought candy was a rare treat for us and so was greatly appreciated. The Sunday school crowd would perform a Christmas Pageant every year and I was always a little disappointed because I wanted to be Joseph or at least one of the Wise Men but I was always assigned to one of the Sheppard roles.

I remember one Christmas, an unusual thing happened which added a little drama to what would otherwise have been a routine event. A row of our small Sunday school children dressed as angels and carrying candles were parading up the isle when one little boy became distracted and failed to keep a proper distance behind the little girl in front of him. His candle ignited her hair which apparently was covered with hair spray and her hair went up in a flash. Fortunately the fire was so brief she suffered no injury. The practice of using real lit candles was understandability thereafter discontinued.

When we were young we believed Santa brought all the gifts and the Christmas tree so it must have been easy to perpetrate a fraud on us. One year the folks must have been planning to be gone on Christmas Eve and needed Santa to show up a few days early. We had just come in from school on a sunny, snow free afternoon and found the folding doors between the dining room and the living room closed. These doors normally were never closed but before we could question the difference, my mother immediately exclaimed, "I hear sleigh bells. Maybe Santa was here."

Opening the folding doors to the living room revealed our Christmas tree all set up with our gifts under it. I remember wondering how Santa's sleigh could have been pulled across our snow free gravel road without making a loud grating noise. I don't know why I never questioned how Santa got into the house through the four inch diameter stovepipe leading from our coal stove to the chimney.

Other instances of deception by my parents were making old toys disappear for a few months before Christmas and then, sporting a new coat of paint, they would reappear under the Christmas tree. We had a small child size table and chairs that went through that transformation a couple of times and on one occasion, my sister's doll reappeared with a new face and clothes. I guess my folks were doing the best they could for us. When we were older and no longer believed in Santa, the game now was to find, before Christmas, any gifts which might be hidden in the house. Apparently having limited funds, my mother would ask if we wanted a lot of small inexpensive gifts or one large expensive one. Also now we would put up the tree a few weeks before Christmas and wrapped gifts would accumulate under it.

My folks used the same small artificial Christmas tree for my entire childhood. The size and appearance of its main trunk always reminded me of a cigar. Its wound-wire limbs were only about a foot long at the bottom and its total height was about four feet. Every year we would decorate it with strings of popcorn and a few new ornaments in addition to whatever had survived from the preceding year.

Winter and snow could also be a source of imaginative entertainment. On occasion, my sister Janet and I would invent games of endurance such as who could run the furthest away from the house and back while barefooted in the snow. One of our games precipitated an injury, about which I will always feel guilty. We were playing in the yard and had made a snowman. I don't remember the actual game we were playing but in the execution of it, Janet somehow taunted me and then ran and hid behind the snowman. I had a child's play broom that I had been using as a throwing spear and I playfully threw it at the snowman thinking it would only harmlessly impale itself. Unfortunately, the broom handle completely penetrated the snowman and exiting its far side, hit Janet in the left eye. Luckily she did not lose her vision but it did put a small cut in her eyelid which our local doctor tried to repair with a piece of tape. To prevent recurring bleeding, she was unable to open her eye for a few days. This was finally brought under control by Maw who applied a compress with something called Painpaint. I remember this was used for a variety of ailments but I have no idea what it was made of. Janet had to wear an eye patch like a pirate to school for a few weeks until it healed. This turned out to be inadequate and left her with a small permanent scar.

Not to minimize her injuries but she does have fewer scars than I have. My first permanent scar she inflicted on me when she was about four years old. Somehow she managed to lift a carpenter's hammer high enough to let it tip over and fall on my head. That small scar is still there above my right ear. The scars over my left eye and on the top of my head were stupidly self-inflicted while playing in our barn. The first was the result of panicking while playing some sort of chase game. To escape my pursuer, I jumped out of the hayloft onto the barn floor below and accidentally struck my head above my left eye on the iron wheel of our hay rake. This put a small crack in my eyebrow ridge which is still there to this day. The other scar, on the top of my head, came about as the result of another game played in the barn with my friend Don. The short version is I was trying to pull him out of the haymow by hanging upside down on the end of a rope he was holding above me. Rather than being pulled off, he simply let go and I fell upside down six feet into hay manger below.

Yet another occasion for my parents to see me coming in all blooded. My family, however having an early pioneer independent philosophy, believed if it isn't life threatening there was no need to see a doctor. We just didn't think it was necessary. Except for my birth and two bouts with scarlet fever, I managed to avoid seeing a doctor for the first eighteen years of my life.

As was the custom at that time, children raised on farms

were part of the work force and, from an early age, shared the load equally with the adults. And so it was with us. In the house, Janet and I would share the duty of washing and drying dishes and, to make the job less boring, we would practice our two-part harmony, singing simple folk songs.

Generally though, Janet's daily duties were in the house and mine were chores in the barn. In addition to feeding the chickens and pigs, milking the cows was always an inescapable necessity.

Because our farm was small, we did not have the luxury of permanent pastures for the cows but would move them from one field of convenience to another. Sometimes this would be an area seeded with alfalfa specifically for them and at other times they were allowed to scavenge in a recently harvested field. These different areas were defined by enclosing them with an electric fence. Consisting of nothing but a single wire attached to glass insulators on light metal post, these fences were easily moved from one place to another as the need arose. The nature of cows is to imprint their environment in their feeble minds so very quickly a well worn path to and from the barn would form along the new fence location. The interesting part of this is, when the fence was moved to another part of the field, the cows would still for a long time walk in their original path along the now absent fence. Sometimes I would try to drive them into the newly opened area but they just wouldn't go. Pretty dumb I thought but not as dumb as I was on one occasion. I decided to pee on this electric fence.

I don't know why I did it.

I just did it.

I never did it again.

I don't know how young I was when I started milking but I had to be strong enough to exert enough pressure on the cow's teat to expel the milk. Milking was made easier with a type of salve called Bag Balm we applied to the cow's teats as a lubricant. This salve had the consistency of Petroleum Jelly and could only be removed from our hands by washing with an abrasive like Lava Hand Soap. Bag Balm can still be found for sale and everyone in my family still has in on hand even though the label on the container warns against its use by humans.

We have found its antiseptic and healing powers to be unchallenged and I still use it to this day.

Our cows were trained to respond to being called to the barn at milking time and a call in the form of a loud "Soooo Baaaws" would bring them running for their reward of ground grain. Our milking stalls were assigned to individual cows and they always knew which one was theirs. The stalls were constructed with alternating narrow and wide wooden slots through which each cow could put her head and eat out of the manger. All the cows but one knew that the wide slot was the only usable one. The single exception would occasionally manage to get her head through the narrow slot and then couldn't get it back out again. This was a constant source of irritation for me as I would have to manually manipulate her head to free her and on one occasion, I lost my temper and banged her over the head with a shovel. I don't think it cured her and all I accomplished was forever feeling guilty for having knocked off one of her horns. Looking back, I wonder why the idea of closing the narrow slots with an additional board never occurred to me. All ten of our milk cows had names of which I can now only remember Betty, Brownie, and Frisky. One of the small rewards gleaned from the job of milking was squirting a stream of milk from the cows' teat into our kittens loudly meowing upturned faces. They didn't seem to mind this delivery system as milk anyway you can get it is better than none.

When I was around fourteen, the laborious task of hand milking was eliminated when we installed a milking machine. This reduced the time and labor associated with this chore but it did nothing to change the inflexible daily schedule of milking every morning and evening.

In order to keep the cows producing as much milk as possible, we would let them breed as soon as they were ready after previously giving birth. So with their nine month gestation period, that would give us a new calf about once a year. About two months before the expected new arrival, her milk would have decreased so we would let her "go dry." This means we would milk only once a day for a bit and then every other day for a while. She would finally get the idea and stop producing.

We would let the new calf nurse for a few days until the cow stops making the special milk especially designed for the newborn. Now here the fun begins. How do you teach an animal to look down and drink out of a bucket when its every instinct tells it to look up and drink from a teat? You use subterfuge. You first offer a finger as a substitute teat and while the beast is thusly engaged, slowly force its head down into the milk and calf formula in a bucket. Diligence is required here as a calf is designed to butt its head if it feels there is an inadequate flow coming from its mother. Many buckets have gone flying due to this nasty habit. When the calves were older and starting to graze, we used them as lawnmowers in the barnyard. Using a length of light chain, they were tied to stakes around which they could graze a circular area. This worked well except occasionally they would wind themselves around the stake until they were snubbed up tight and could no longer move. Unwinding calves was just another regular job in the summer.

We raised one or two pigs every year only for our own consumption. Pigs will eat almost anything which made them a handy disposal system for all our kitchen waste. Even dishwater was included in the mix and they seemed to really like that. Of course we supplemented their diet with grain and occasionally a little coal. I think the carbon in coal aided their digestion and they would crunch it down with everything else. I never liked the idea of butchering them and one year this necessary action was particularly sad for me. On that fateful morning after everything had been made ready, my father took his 22 caliber rifle and headed toward the pigpen. The pig, seeing him coming, ran toward the fence thinking it was going to be fed. Stopping at the fence and obligingly looking up at my father, it seemed to be saying "Well?" I am sure the poor thing didn't expect what it got. What happened this time was even sadder than it usually is. When my father shot it between the eyes, it just blinked and had to be shot a second time before it fell to the ground. I admit I like eating meat as much as anyone but I prefer to take the cowards approach and have it rendered into unrecognizable portions before I am exposed to it.

When I was about twelve years old, my father enclosed the

where we could raise chickens. This second floor room was accessed by a three foot wide stairway along the outside wall of the milking room. At the top was a small landing with the door to the chicken room on the right and a catwalk leading to the other haymow on the left. All the feed for the chickens was manually carried up these stairs in large buckets weighing about thirty pounds. I can't believe it now but I was strong enough at that age to accomplish this much heavy lifting.

In order to start this operation, we would buy newly hatched chicks from a commercial establishment whose only business was hatching eggs into chicks. The chicks would be delivered in shallow corrugated cardboard containers resembling large Pizza boxes. Through the dozens of ventilation holes in the top, the incessant peeping of the occupants could always be heard. This gentle small sound is a perfect match to their physical appearance. There is nothing cuter than a baby chicken and nothing grosser than a teenager which has lost its baby down and is without feathers.

After a few years my father eliminated the middleman and constructed a small incubator in our basement for hatching our own chicks. The process of hatching is not always a perfect process and nature sometimes makes mistakes. A small percent of the eggs would not yield a complete hatch. My father would not try to save a chick still partial enclosed in its shell and would throw them out with the empty shells. It always bothered me to hear them peeping in the pile of refuse in the field back of our house.

My father also had constructed a small building we called The Brooder House. The baby chicks were kept here under a heated hood for about six weeks. They were then moved to the chicken room in the barn.

One night here in this Brooder House, a small life and death drama was played out. My father had just returned home in the evening from some Church function and, still wearing his dress suit, went out to check on the baby chickens. Inside he discovered a large mouse eating the chicken feed and when he tried to kill it by stomping on it in a corner, the poor panicked creature ran up inside his pants leg. Making a desperate grab at the mouse, he acted with an uncontrollable reflex and squashed the mouse in his fist. I don't know how they explained that one to the cleaners.

Some of the time we would raise Broilers for the meat market and at other times, we raised chickens for their eggs.

When raised them for the latter, there was additional work involved. It is not commonly known but chickens, given the opportunity, will turn to cannibalism. Occasionally a heavy laying hen will bleed under her tail and when this starts all the other chickens will pick at the bloody area and if not stopped they will eventually kill their victim. To prevent this from happening, we would install on each chicken a sort of mechanical beak shield. This was a device which would swing out of the way when their heads were down while eating but would make it impossible to grab anything with their heads raised. This shield was held in place with a cotter pin through their nostrils. Attaching one of these devises on every chicken was always performed after dark when they are asleep and easy to catch. It seems to me this was a very barbaric but necessary business.

A final thought about chickens. For some reason unknown to me, my father was the locally designated chicken vaccination expert. Even now after all these years, if driving through the country after dark and I see a small white light coming from a barn or shed in the distance, I am reminded of all the times I helped my father vaccinate all our neighbors chickens. Always at night with only the light from one small kerosene lantern, he would apply the vaccine on a bare spot under each chicken's wing. It was my job to collect the sleeping birds from their roosts and then return them to their perch while keeping track so as not to miss one.

These routine farm tasks were not particularly unpleasant but their ridged inflexibility made any spontaneous interruption impossible. They required attention morning and evening, seven days a week, fifty two weeks a year. For years after I left the farm, every day near sundown, I would still get an apprehensive feeling that there was something I must be doing.

When we did manage get away for a few days, it was for a

visit at my maternal grandmother's house sixty miles away in Fremont. We looked forward to these rare visits with great anticipation and excitement. My father would spend an entire day servicing our 1935 Chevy preparing for this long journey.

On the way, Janet and I would play a game we called oil wells. Sitting in the back seat of the car, this was a contest to see who could sight the most oil well pumps on our respective side of the road. We didn't seem to mind that the number of wells probably didn't change from one trip to the next, as these trips were so infrequent we would forget the results anyway. When we sighted the first billboards several miles from the edge of town, our excitement could hardly be contained.

Grandma's house was a wonderful place filled with the odors of baked goods and fried chicken. She also had a refrigerator from which we would steal ice from its small trays. In those early years, we had no electricity on the farm so luxuries like ice in the summer were beyond imagination.

Do to the infrequency of our visits, my Mother's three sisters, Aunt Kathryn, Aunt Harriet, and Aunt Aretha who all lived nearby would always show up and prepare a Thanksgiving style dinner. On these occasions, everyone sat around eating and talking into the late afternoon, only leaving the table to replenish or re-heat the food. I really preferred listening to the women's conversations as their gossip was always accompanied with a lot of animation and laughter. They would reminisce about the past and tell stories of their youth. One story I remember was their adolescent belief that their bodies were just hollow vessels filled with blood and if they would jump up and down after eating they could make room for more food. They were also sort of naughty and would tease me about my so called love life.

The only negative part of my visit was trying to sleep with the unaccustomed sounds and lights of the city. Cars passing on the street in front of the house cast moving shadows on the walls and made rumbling sounds which, being completely absent in my home in the country, fed all my childish fears of the dark.

This city was, compared to our small country town, a place of limitless diversity and industry. The Sandusky River, running through the middle of the city, was crossed by a bridge which connected the residential side of town with the more interesting commercial district. I found walking across that bridge to be both exciting and frightening. Even though the gaps in the concrete railing were small, I still had an uneasy feeling I might somehow manage to accidentally fall through into the swirling muddy water below. Hurrying across this bridge would bring me to the junction of two streets and the railroad tracks which ran parallel with the river. The railroad station close by was always filled with food venders, shoe-shine stands and people just lounging about.

This was always a place of wonder and excitement for me as it was so unlike anything back home. The tempting odors of popcorn and roasting peanuts were everywhere but I would resist buying anything as I was saving my meager funds for my favorite, a German hot-dog with sauerkraut served by a vender just up the street from the station. It was here I had my first in person exposure to an individual belonging to another race. Of course I had seen many Negroes in the movies but this was different. I think my reaction was mostly one of curiosity.

From here the main street ran on up the hill from the river toward the part of town where my cousin Larry lived. He and I would ride our bicycles down that hill at full speed and arriving at the bottom without slowing down, we could only hope to avoid any vehicular or train cross traffic. Traffic in those days was not what it is now.

Larry and I would also go swimming in the municipal pool and it was here one summer that I fell hopelessly in love again. All I can remember about her now is she had big beautiful black eyes and long black hair. Being only in my teens at the time, all I could do about it was a lot of wistful daydreaming. I met her every day at the swimming pool and when I told her I was going home the next day, she gave me a small pink perfume laden plastic heart. I kept this memento under my pillow at home long after its essence had faded. If only these bitter sweet feelings of youth could be relived later in life.

On one of these trips to Grandma's, we had the good fortune to visit a resort on Lake Erie named Cedar Point. This was the absolute highlight of my life to that point. The sight, smell and feel of the sand and water are permanently etched in my memory. My step grandfather had a very small house trailer parked in the park by the. beach and some of us slept in it and the rest in a small tent close by. This park also hosted a penny arcade from which music could be heard day and night. I still remember a few of the lyrics of one of the songs being constantly broadcast.

"Ooooh the doors swing in and the doors swing out.
While some pass in and others pass out.
Da -??????- da.
Behind those swinging doors."

I delighted in shuffling across its sand covered wooden floor, as the feel of its smoothness and texture was very pleasant on my field hardened bare feet.

That week I stayed in the water so much each day, my skin turned wrinkled and blue. This experience forever convinced me that playing on a beach next to any large body of water was eminently preferable to chopping weeds in a hot dusty corn field.

Unfortunately though, instead of lounging on a beach, I was back on our farm. Here I spent many hot sultry summer days trudging up and down in the soybean, wheat, oat, and corn fields, waging an unending war against poor plants that had the misfortune of having been labeled "weeds." A common joke was, "If you cut down one weed, twenty would show up for its funeral." I personally had nothing against them but apparently the locals believed having a few weeds showing in a grain field was as slovenly as being unshaven in church.

Being barefooted most of the time in the summer, I had to contend with a weed called we called Kanda Thistles. I think their real name is Canadian Thistles. This plant was the most prolific and hardy one I have ever seen. Sporting a solid covering of super sharp needles on all their leaves and at first growing flat on the ground, they could lay down a solid impenetrable carpet which made walking through, even with calloused feet, something to absolutely avoid if possible. This plant flourished in freshly cultivated earth and was, among all others, the leader in resuscitation. What made it worse was if it had been cut by the cultivator, the dead dried stems and leaves were even more dangerous than the live ones. The best we could hope for in the eradicating department was fighting it to a draw.

Another common weed in this part of the country is the Milkweed. This plant had no fear of death and proudly displayed its large flat green leaves high above the surrounding grain stems. Being single plants growing at widely spaced intervals, their unpopularity was more cosmetic than a threat to the crops. When cut, their stems would exude a pure white sticky foul tasting sap from which their name was derived. On maturity, they produced a large seed pod containing hundreds of seeds, each attached to an explosion of fine filaments that could carry them on the wind to distant futile ground. Their frequent recurrent growth did however serve one useful purpose. The constant need for their removal provided a handy excuse for finding something for idle hands to do. I was all too frequently given the honor of pursuing their eradication.

As the eldest, I was given an opportunity to do many more things than my brother Richard who was seven years my junior. I started driving our tractor when I was nine and our Model T Ford truck at about twelve years of age. In the beginning, I could not reach the tractor clutch with my foot while sitting on the seat and I asked my father if he would move the seat a little forward but he declined saying I would grow into it. So for a few years I would engage the clutch while standing up and then take a step backwards and sit down on the seat. Like any kid would, I preferred driving over walking any time. However sitting for hours on a hard cold steel tractor seat can get pretty old too so I would frequently alternate between sitting and standing. Preparing the fields for planting was the type of tractor driving I did the most. Either plowing or disking, it was basically the same boring activity. Up and back from one side of the field to the other. The only entertainment available was not slowing the tractor at the end of the field during the turn. Even though the tractor wasn't capable of any real speed, doing an about face under full power could be exciting.

Many farm activities involved various kinds of hard physical labor. I couldn't see much advantage in hard work and avoided it whenever I could. My father once said to me, "You will never have to worry about having fleas as they won't stay on anything that's dead."

On one occasion he might have been better off had he not asked for my assistance because this set up a condition which would plague him for as long as he had our old 1935 Chevy.

He had asked me to hold the funnel while he poured gas into car's tank. Somehow I happened to be eating peanuts at the time so naturally a peanut fell from my mouth into the funnel and was immediately washed into the tank. From that day on, at totally random and unexpected times, that peanut would get into the gas tank outlet and shut everything down. Whereupon my father would have to disconnect the gas line under the hood and with his mouth, blow this obstruction back out of the way. I wouldn't have blamed him if he had disowned me at that point.

We owned a small section of land we called The New Ground and I did enjoy working there. This was an area, now cleared of trees and brush, which had only recently been woodland. We were preparing the land for farming and in so doing; much time was spent digging out the buried roots and stumps. These were then gathered into large piles for burning. My whole family would be involved in this activity. As we were some distance from the house, we brought with us, a one dish meal carried in a large metal pot. This was usually beef stew which was my favorite. At lunch time, the pot would then be placed next to the burning stumps for heating. Sitting around the fire and eating with the smell of wood smoke adding extra flavor to our food was always a very pleasant break in the days work.

It seemed we could not find and completely remove all the roots so every time we tried to plow with the tractor, we would inevitably catch on something we had missed. Having to stop and cut the snags out of the plow made this slow going. This clearing activity was done as filler in the normal farm routine. At harvest time, this new ground cornfield would be picked by hand and the entire family would participate here also. Ears were pulled off the stalks and after removing the husks, were thrown into the bed of our truck. As we moved up and down the corn rows, it was my privilege to jump in and out of the truck and the drive it a few feet at a time to keep up. This was one of the rare times when I would volunteer as I loved driving the truck even if it was only for a few feet at a time.

Life in the summer wasn't all about work. Mid summer evenings did provide a brief acception to the routine. This was time of year when the twilight would be filled with millions of tiny lights which would appear for a second and then fade just a quickly. This was season for Fireflies or Lighting Bugs as we called them. These benign little creatures used a cold chemical reaction in their thorax to produce a short pulse of iridescent bright yellow light. I believe this was used for mating purposes. I can't believe there isn't a person alive who, having lived as a child in an area where these insects existed, did not run madly about in the twilight trying to capture as many as they could and, hoping to keep the magic alive, save them in a glass jar.

When I was about four years old, my father brought home a small short haired brown and white pudgy terrier puppy and we named her Poochie. She grew up with us and was a member of our household and our constant companion for the entire fourteen years of her life. All dogs are territorial and Poochie was no exception. The only difference was her territory turned out to be our tractor. If we left the tractor in the field over night, she would remain and sleep under it, awaiting our return the next morning. Starting the tractors engine would always initiate much running about and barking. If the engine was started in the barnyard, she would immediately tree every cat and chicken in sight. She never seemed to tire of this game. For some reason, this dog had also decided to live on the edge. When we were plowing, the one large tractor drive wheel would always be running in a freshly opened furrow and Poochie would happily trot along in that opening just inches in front of the ever descending steel lugs on that rotating wheel. This was hair-raising enough but it got worse when she hesitated to examine something of interest. Usually this was a field mouse with enough good sense to be getting out of the way. Somehow Poochie always managed to resume her forward motion in the nick of time and avoided getting squashed as the result of her distraction.

On any farm where there is food for rats, they inevitably will be established in large numbers. Our chicken room built on the second floor of the barn always provided a handy buffet for them. Our only method of rat control was to have Poochie wait on the ground floor by the fresh water pipe that extended from the ground up through the floor above. When the lights in the chicken room were turned on, all the rats ran for the water pipe and slid down like firemen in a firehouse. With our 410 gauge shotgun sticking through a gap at the top of the wall, my father would shoot as many of the descending rats as he could and Poochie would, with a couple shakes, dispatch in rapid succession most of the survivors at the bottom.

Years later we adopted a large short-haired heavy bodied stray dog that showed up one day with bleeding feet and a look of resignation on his face. We could only guess his history but he must have been following someone in a car or truck and finally was no longer able to keep up.

Poochie didn't seem to mind his presence so we decided to keep him. We named him Butch. He was three times bigger than Poochie and had a very sunny disposition and was always ready to play. In winter I decided to make a sled dog team out of the two of them. I had a small coaster sled which I connected to a two-dog harness I had made and after hooking up the dogs, Butch leading in front and Poochie following behind, I attempted conveying my intentions to my team. Butch seemed more interested in riding than pulling and Poochie meanwhile, resisted the whole idea completely and refused to move an inch. I finally made Butch understand what was expected of him by running in front and leading the way but Poochie on the other hand, steadfastly refused to cooperate and was ignominiously dragged, stiff-legged and resolute, along behind. She finally won out and I assigned her to the more dignified role of barking and chasing the sled as we careened down our snow covered road. This was great fun but there was no directional control of Butch, and as a result he would go wherever his interest took him. Usually this was not a problem but on one occasion, a stupid wild rabbit decided to cross the road in front of us and as any dog would, Butch gave chase. A sharp right turn resulted in my falling off into the snow while dog and sled were off chasing the rabbit through the frozen stubble of the oat field.

Another time, I had acquired two small white and brown short haired puppies whose origin is lost in memory but whose demise is not.

One puppy was almost all white with a few brown spots and the other was mostly brown with a few white spots. The brown puppy some how shortly after arriving, fell in our water well pit and landing on a pipe, unhappily did not survive. The other puppy's demise occurred later as the result of a double calamity. This was an extremely black day for me.

I was alone on the farm for the day but being alone was a common event and this day was no different than hundreds of others had been. I was doing my routine chores in the barn when, while feeding our small herd of milk cows, one of the young heifers got pushed onto her back upside down in the watering trough. In her desperate attempts to right herself, she started striking her head repeatedly against the barn wall. I was much too small to be of any help to the poor animal and, if left alone, she would have done a great injury to herself. My only option was to get help from our closest neighbor as soon as possible. I started running down the road toward their house with my half-grown puppy happily running along behind on the opposite side of the road. Using very poor judgment, she decided to cross the road and join me on my side just as a car was passing. Unavoidably, she was struck by the car and killed. With tears streaming down my face, I continued on to our neighbor's house and got him to return with me to rescue our trapped heifer.

We had to tip over the water trough to get her out and on her feet again. Heartbroken, I later retrieved my puppy's body and buried her in our back yard.

Having chores at home every afternoon prevented me from staying after school for basketball or baseball practice and as a result, I was not very popular with the local girls who generally went for the jocks. This condition forced me to look for female companionship in the neighboring communities. I had discovered roller-skating as a natural and effective way to have any semblance of a social life and I took every possible opportunity to do so. The closest roller-skating rink was some ten miles up the road in Napoleon and as I didn't have my own transportation, I was forced to hitch-hike when I went skating. Hitch-hiking in those days was not considered dangerous. At least there was no threat from the local farmers who would give us a ride. We only had to avoid riding with the good natured drinkers who would sometimes fail to stay on the road and end up in the ditch. This happened to me several times and even though there seemed to be an irresistible force which drew them off the road, I don't recall a single accidental death being caused by a drunk driver. Perhaps this was due to the limited speeds the cars were capable of at the time. Pursuing this skating activity did require some ingenuity at times. I recall one Sunday in summer, I wanted to go but my father denied me permission. So I told him I was going for a long hike in the woods. I packed my roller skates and a change of clothing in my back-pack and took a long hike in the woods, only after changing clothes there, I cut through to the main highway and hitch-hiked to Napoleon. After skating I returned the same way I had come and while changing back into my old clothes, I became extremely paranoid thinking maybe my father was looking for me. Fortunately my fears were groundless and nothing was said but I still felt guilty for a long time.

The main problem with hitch-hiking was the uncertainty of getting a ride. This manifested itself one day in early winter when after skating; I had lingered too long at the youth hangout at the edge of town and got a late start on the road home. The temperature had dropped below freezing and I was wearing only a light topcoat with no hat at the time. As traffic was light to nonexistent, I got quite cold waiting for a ride. Finally a farmer picked me up in his old Model A Ford and even though he had no heat in the cab, I was grateful to be getting any kind of a ride. My benefactor was going only as far as the city limits of Holgate and that left me with a three mile walk the rest of the way home. The weather was broken overcast with a light breeze as I started on foot for my house. During an occasional break in the clouds, the moon would light the road enough for me to see the fine snow swirling across the road in front of me. About half way to the house I started feeling tired and thoughts of sitting down and resting entered my mind. I knew these were the first signs of freezing so I was able to resist the temptation and kept moving.

Of course I made it home but it was close.

The transportation problem improved somewhat when my buddies, Dan and Don, turned sixteen and got their drivers licenses, I already had a work related license which had allowed me to drive in farm related activities. At least now my buddies and I could trade off borrowing our fathers' cars and team up on dates and other nefarious activities. Don and I frequently went skating together and spent many evenings cruising for girls in the neighboring towns. There is a strange transformation that occurs to a young female when she puts on a skating skirt with skating shoes. She is immediately changed from old ordinary into the sexiest image you have ever seen. This was a time of hormones running amuck and I would instantly fall in love with any girl foolish enough to go on a date with me. The tendency to always be falling in love with anyone who would stand still got me in a lot of trouble all through my life. Instead of having nice innocent affairs, I would always do the right thing and marry the girl.

# Chapter Eleven    The Missing Years

This section details my life after my return from duty in North Africa. I can't promise you much excitement or pathos in this period. Sometime I had to just let life happen without much thought or direction.

The management at Squantum must have noticed my lack of enthusiasm as I was soon transferred back to where it had all started six years earlier. My new assignment at Glenview Navel Air Station was across the street from where it had all started in Boot Camp.

I ended up assigned to the standby emergency crew on the four PM to midnight shift. I think this shift was created just to get some of the crew spread out and relieve the congestion during the day. Occasionally a plane would report a malfunction of some kind but as there were no stockrooms open at that hour, we could do nothing but refer the problem to the day shift. Sometimes the Marine Sergeant in charge would simply say at muster "Don't beat the day shift out the gate." There was always a Poker game going and the lounge room always provided food in the form of a home-made stew we called Holostros (phonetic spelling); the taste and consistency of which constantly changed with time.

As a result of working the evening shift, I was able to manage a civilian job during the day. Slowly my state of mind was improving. Maybe it was the nearness of my release from the Navy or it could have been the fact that I was able to take a civilian job during the day that created the illusion that I was already out of the Navy.

I worked that spring and summer at the Glenview Country Club as a Greens Keeper, mowing greens early in the morning with seeding and general trimming fairways later in the day. The country club also hired collage girls on summer break to work in the dining room and kitchen. I had casual dates with several of the girls that summer and it remains in memory as a very pleasant contrast with the inevitable cold miserable winter weather which always follows in that part of the country.

Didn't I warn you that this part would be dull?

Honorably discharged from the Navy, I was now, for the first time in my life, completely free to do whatever I wanted for as long as I wanted. My first eighteen years had been under the control of my family and the following seven years had been at the mercy of the Navy. So now what to do?

Lets leap-frog from here to a month in Pasadena Ca. working as an electronic assembler, to delivering milk and butter door to door in the middle of the winter in Randolph Mass.

Here fate saw fit to rescue me from my own stupidity. I slipped on an icy second floor landing and took a header down the stairs. Suffered nothing more serious than a hyper-extended elbow, I ended up with my arm in a cast which made working impossible. This qualified me for workman's compensation payments of thirty-five dollars a week.

After surveying my options, I reasoned I might starve, but if I did, I wanted to do it where it was warm. So after my cast was removed and I got my first check, I headed south with thirty five dollars in my pocket and Miami Florida in my mind.

The date was December 13, 1956.

The drive south was uneventful except one time while getting gas at a filling station, I was approached by a young man who had noticed my guitar in the back seat and inquired if I was a musician. After a short conversation, we found we were from the same part of Ohio. He was living with two other friends in a small trailer and only one of them had a half day job unloading mail from the daily train. They shared their meager brown bread and beans with me and I felt obligated to help them out but being even poorer than they were, I was unable to do so. Still they invited me to stay with them as long as I wanted. I thankfully declined their offer and was soon back on my way again. I arrived at the outskirts of Palm Beach on a Friday afternoon with a quarter of a tank of gas and only forty cents in my pocket. I decided, given my limited resources, this had to be as far as I could go. It was late in the afternoon and I found a spot in an empty parking lot and holed up for the night. I hadn't slept much on the way down so I was grateful for the chance to just relax for awhile and was able to get a fairly good night sleep in the car.

The next morning the weather was intermittent small showers with bright sunshine in between. Ducking into doorways to keep dry, I spent the day walking around the town soliciting information in regard to employment. Everyone was friendly enough but I acquired no usable job information. I wasn't concerned for I had absolute faith something would turn up. This unconscious independent attitude probably accounted for the fact that calling my folks and asking them for a little help never entered my mind. I think by this time I had completely restored my natural cheerful and optimistic view of the future. What the Hell? I wasn't too hungry, the sun was shining and I still had a few cigarettes left so things weren't that bad.

Monday morning, while looking through a discarded newspaper, I spotted an employment agency ad which looked encouraging. The kindly gray haired lady who was taking applications waved their regular fifty cent fee and signed me up.

Now I faced a really big hurdle. Because of the large population of the rich and famous living in Palm Beach, the police want to know who is in town. This meant a police working permit is required to get a job. To get this permit, one must have a local address. To get a local address one must have money. To get money one must have a job. You see the problem. By good fortune, leaving my spare tire and wheel as collateral, I was able to talk a restaurant owner into lending me twenty dollars. Now I rented a sleeping room for seventeen dollars a week and got my police work permit. My first interview provided by the agency was for a house-man at the Colony Hotel. The manager there asked if my goal in life was to be a house-man and I replied "No, but part of my goal is to eat." He laughed and then inquired about my Navy experience and could I swim? I assured him I was eminently qualified and he countered with the offer of a job as life guard, swimming instructor and pool-boy.

Now who would turn down a job like that?

Every morning after raising the flag by the pool, I would make my own breakfast in the Hotel kitchen and take my silver service breakfast tray out to a pool-side table where I could read the morning paper while I ate

.

My duties consisted mostly of retrieving wet towels from the lounge chairs around the pool and ordering drinks for the guests. These chairs were not to be reserved but I could always get a big tip if I made one look occupied by leaving a wet towel on it. Luckily this job included daily tips so I was able to pay my rent without having to wait for my first paycheck. One steady source of tips came from an upper-middle-aged woman who would show up every afternoon for a swim. She would enter in the shallow water and then swim toward the deep end. When only about six feet from safety, she would start to flounder and this created an opportunity for me to be a hero and pull her out. Every day this little routine would get me a five dollar tip.

Just having a lot of money though, doesn't free a person from earthly afflictions. This lady would also regularly tip the house-man who would, with appropriate gear, routinely follow her about in the hotel. Sadly she had a continence problem.

Another regular of mine, an gentleman by the name of Morgan, was over ninety years old and routinely bragged about having oysters flown in for him every day. He would announce "I'm in really good health except for hardening of the arteries but what the Hell, you have to die from something."

My regular tip income was adequate but it didn't compare with what could be made in a different part of the hotel. I am referring to the bartender who worked evenings in the hotel's lounge. It was reported that in appreciation for his exceptional service to a particular lady customer, he was given a new Thunderbird for Christmas.

Another elderly guest at the Hotel had a full time valet and driver named Carl who always accompanied him wherever he went. This was two men living one man's life. I don't understand why anyone would want someone else to do all of life's everyday ordinary things for them. This old man was not an invalid but just apparently chose to be as helpless at seventy as he had been when he was two. When the old man went for a swim, Carl would be waiting with a towel to wrap around him the instant he exited the water.

During their visits to the pool, Carl would sit and talk with me and after awhile he became quite friendly. He occasionally had free time and having unlimited access to all the "in" places in town, he made a great guide. At his invitation, I got to see much more than I could have afforded on my own. I realized finally, he was gay and was courting me. Without insulting him, I managed to let him know my interests lay elsewhere.

In fact they lay with another occupant of the apartment house where I was staying. This was a young German immigrant girl working as a seamstress for the upper crust in Palm Beach. She spoke English with a charming accent that reminded me of Marlene Dietrich. I was impressed when she told me she had learned to speak English in just six months by watching Television.

Sometimes, just to have something to do in the evening, I worked with a valet service parking cars for a popular exclusive nightclub. Not that it made me any richer, I did have the privilege of parking Jack (as he was known at that time) Kennedy's and Peter Lawford's cars.

This job gave me much needed exercise because not having a real parking area, we were forced to park the cars anywhere on the street we could find. Sometimes that meant running at full speed for several blocks to retrieve a car.

At the end of the winter season in Florida, I decided to visit my folks who were now living on a small farm near Bill Clinton's home town of Hope, Arkansas.

Feeling a little guilty for having been away for so many years, I now felt I should stay closer to my family for awhile. Needing to make a living, I scanned a regional map looking for the closest city which would have the best employment possibilities. It turned out Dallas Texas was just eighty miles down the road with a good interconnecting state highway. This was an ideal destination.

There was no way I could have know how profoundly my future would be affected by my decision to give this place a try.

I found in the Dallas Morning News help wanted ads, many listings of help wanted at Chance Vaught Aircraft in Grand Prairie. This town was a close suburb of Dallas and conveniently out of the main crowded metropolitan area. Using my Navy experience as a reference, I landed a job on the Regulas Missile assembly line.

I spent the first week installing long bundles of wire while hanging like a bat through the access in the top of the missile. The second week I decided to look for something a little less acrobatic. Luckily I was reassigned to the Electronics Development Lab. This turned out to be a significant professional identity change for me. I was no longer an electrician but now an electronics technician. This job was more title than performance as all we did was build prototype electronic "black boxes."

I became an expert with a soldering iron and little else. But it was interesting and I enjoyed working there. After about six months, I transferred to the 4PM to Midnight shift. This move made it possible for me to go to nearby Arlington State Collage during the day.

I had taken and passed my GED while in the Navy and passing the collage entrance exam was not difficult. I had thought long and hard about what I wanted to do for the rest of my life and had come to the conclusion that a really good life could be had as a Doctor of Veterinarian Medicine. I thought as a Veterinarian, I would have an unlimited choice of where I could live. They are found after all, everywhere from the smallest towns to the largest cities. However while standing in the registration line at the Collage, I was thumbing through the course book looking at all the other classes offered and by the time I got to the registrars table, I had changed my Major from Doctor of Veterinarian Medicine to Music Appreciation.

Another smart move as the last thing I needed then was to be starting on another long drawn out project chosen with logic instead of emotion.

At that time, Chance Vaught had three shifts working and with that many people available twenty-four hours a day, most of the local businesses remained open around the clock. Even the movie theater played extra features until three in the morning. Being a night person, I would not go to bed until around six in the morning. I arranged to have all my collage classes in the afternoon so I could sleep until noon. The six hours between six AM and noon was all the sleep I ever needed. In the summer the weather would be very pleasant at night and when there was a full moon, I would go for a sail on Lake Lewisville in the small Sun Fish sail boat I bought. This part of Texas is very dry with no rain in the summer and the absence of dampness and dew at night made camping out in the open at the lake a popular activity.

Luckily, I had become friends with Ben, the fry cook at the local family restaurant where I took all my meals and having common interests (mainly girls); we decided to rent a house together. Ben was an interesting person who believed on acting on impulse. He married a young lady one weekend after only knowing her for one day. His stated reason was because she had a Ford Convertible and a new television set.

Small wonder, a week later they were separated.

This restaurant was a hangout for a lot of the young adults, giving me an opportunity to make many new friends and being the room-mate of the cook meant I didn't have to pay for anything. It was here I met, wooed, and won my second wife, Connie. We started dating and as so often happens, this leads to living together for a while. We finally got married to legitimize our relationship and I should have known better but by now my attitude toward marriage was completely casual. Connie was a sweet, loving and tolerant person who should have had better luck.

During this period, I had developed a serious interest in Hypnoses and I became quite an expert at it. Many of my friends, for a variety of reasons, wanted me to practice on them. Stopping smoking and help with collage studies were popular subjects. Once I was with a small group which included a mother with her teenage daughter and I was hypnotizing the daughter with everyone else watching. Halfway along, one of the observers nudged my arm and pointed to the mother who was supposed to be just watching, as deep in hypnoses as her daughter. So now I had two of them under at the same time and had to refer to them by name.

I had one rule that I would not change. I would not suggest anything that would make the subject look foolish. This was done for entertainment by many practitioners on television at the time and this always angered me. I was deeply involved in the practice at that time but after awhile I found it was also extremely taxing and when asked to do it at other times later in my life, I found I just didn't have the energy needed to perform adequately.

Well nothing good ever lasts forever and this was no exception. Chance Vaught lost their government contracts and had to layoff many of their workers. In a union shop like this, the layoffs come from the bottom up so we with the least time in service were the first to go.

Not finding another suitable job immediately, I bought a medium size truck and spent a couple of months cutting and hauling pulp wood from my folk's farm in Arkansas. This woodland was formally a cotton farm but was now covered with second growth Loblolly Pine. These trees were grown all through the South to supply pulp wood for the paper industry.

Now here I encountered an affliction completely new to me. I was being constantly plagued by a local parasite called chiggers. A chigger bite was really the blood sucking larva stage of a mite which would create a welt much larger than a mosquito bite and would itch intensely for several days.

My initial introduction to them occurred while Connie and I were visiting the folks one weekend. We had taken a walk through the woods and got carried away by the moment and make love in the leaves under the trees. On our way back to Dallas the next day, we broke out in itchy welts all over our bodies and not knowing the real cause, we thought the car was full of hungry mosquitoes. I no longer remember how we were informed about the source of our misery.

I found the only protection from these parasites was a concoction made from Vaseline and sulfur powder which was applied to all exposed areas of the body. This was very messy but necessary while working in the woods.

For some strange nostalgic reason at that time, I contemplated building a house on a small rise up the road from the main house and after converting the land into pasture, raise a small herd of beef cattle. I'm sure if I had acted on that impulse, I would have regretted it later because something unimagined at that time, was waiting for me in my future.

Back in Dallas and sanity, I answered an ad in the paper for a temporary contract position as a printed circuit designer at Texas Instruments. I had some experience designing circuits at my previous employer and I thought I could bluff enough to get this job. I was so ignorant I didn't know exactly what a Printed Circuit Designer was. At my interview at Texas Instruments I was given a small schematic diagram and a drawing template of several different electronic components and told to make a drawing representing the layout of a small printed circuit board. It turned out their title of Printed Circuit Designer should have been more accurately been labeled Printed Circuit Layout.

I couldn't believe that was all they wanted.

Five years later, I was still at Texas Instruments. I had been on one temporary job after another at various times and in various departments all that time. I worked as a Mechanical Design Draftsman, Electronics Technician, Schematic Draftsman, Integrated Circuit Designer and Printed Circuit Designer.

This was a time of unlimited opportunities for learning. The Integrated Circuit industry was in its infancy and an experienced work force was being trained on the fly. As soon as I was finished with one project, I would immediately be moved to another. On one of these assignments, I ended up in Attleboro Mass. installing an electronic temperature controller on a strip welding machine. This device was created to weld three thin sheets of metal together to form the base sheet from which our Quarters are struck. This was the material which gave the copper edge to the Quarters at that time. Here, I got a small taste for what life could be like for other less fortunate people. This facility consisted entirely of row after row of stamping machines all pounding away at the same time. The noise level in this room made any voice communication absolutely impossible. We used hand signals and if the need to talk became absolutely necessary, we would retire to an adjoining sound proof office. I believe being subjected to that much noise for any extended period of time would be a real health hazard.

Somewhere in this period an opportunity for fame and fortune presented itself. Our local television station advertised auditions for the lead male role in a proposed television series. This show was to be built on the exploits of a character called "The Texan."

I of course, auditioned for the part. The first audition was only a walk on with name and age stated for an appearance and voice check. After making it through the first cut, I was given a two line script and told to return the next day.

Wonder upon wonders, I made it past the second reading as well and was given a much longer script including a love scene with a stand in female. That is as far as I got in the auditions and I never knew if they chose anyone from that cattle call. I know if I had been the one doing the audition, I would have thrown me out bodily. My performance was absolutely awful. Some people are not given the ability to convince an audience they are not acting. Ultimately this project was apparently abandoned. Much to my surprise years later, I saw John Wayne in the movie Hondo, doing exactly the same scene that I had done. I had to do the scene on an empty stage with no props, but he had the distinct advantage of saying these lines while he was saddling a horse.

After about six years, I finally moved my folks off the farm and brought them to Dallas. I had been supporting them for quite awhile and thought it would be easier if they were closer. My father's health was failing and my mother, wanting to help out, got a job as a server in a Jewish delicatessen. This gave her something to do besides sitting at home and worrying. She seemed to really enjoy her job as it got her out of the house and the proprietor's attitude toward their employees gave her a handy source of things to complain about.

About a year after my family moved to Dallas, my father was diagnosed with cancer of the larynx and subsequently had surgery in the M B Anderson clinic in Houston. After his surgery he was living in the Hospital's recovery annex and when they began the surgical reconstruction of his throat, we were optimistic about his eventual recovery. His inability to talk made it necessary for me to develop some ability at lip reading and sometimes this would lead to very humorous exchanges. Once I asked him if he would be able to live at home for a while. My lip reading of his answer came out like this. "I'll have to get baby shit." What he had actually said was, "I'll have to get permission." Have someone mouth the latter and see what I mean.

To avoid having to drive the two hundred fifty miles from Dallas to Houston to visit my father, I decided to make a temporary move. As I had always worked as a "Job Shopper", a name given to professional temporary workers, I was able to immediately get a job in Houston. Even after all my years of steady employment, my father still marveled at the apparent ease with which I could get work. I rented a Motel room by the week and visited him often. I feel we became closer at that time than we ever had been. Still our conversations were about superficial matters and what he really felt, he was not sharing with me. I noticed though, he had developed an intimacy with his fellow cancer afflicted friends at the clinic. I had never seen him make a connection like this with anyone else before. There must have been a shared sense of their common experience that drew them together.

My father had smoked all his life and he saw no reason to try to give it up now. At the first opportunity he had after his surgery, he lit a cigarette but as he no longer had a connection between his mouth and his lungs, he was unable to expel the smoke from his mouth and nose. He told me he had panicked because his reflex of wanting to clear everything out didn't work. This at first was exasperating but he soon learned how to puff with his mouth and get the job done.

Determination triumphed.

The treatment he received was unfortunately not successful and his cancer metastasized into his lungs. He lived for only a year after his original diagnosis.

My father was fifty eight years old when he died.

You would think losing him from a smoking related cancer would have made an impression on me and I would have quit my four packs a day habit, but it didn't. Four packs a day sounds like a lot but in actuality, I didn't ingest that much. I was always working at a desk and I had a cigarette burning all the time in the ashtray instead of me ingesting it. Still it was a very stupid habit.

It would take something allot closer to home to make me quit.

Back in Dallas, I hooked up with a start up contract service company called Micropac.

It was then my younger brother Richard showed up on my doorstep. After serving eleven years in the Air Force Band and having no marketable skills outside of music, he was at a severe disadvantage when it came to finding a job in the High Tech world. Luckily I was farmed out as an Integrated Circuit Designer at Texas Instruments at the time so I bootlegged him out on the job with me and gave him these instructions. "This end of the pencil makes the lines and the other end rubs them out. Keep your eyes and ears open and your mouth shut." From this simple beginning he built a very successful twenty year career in the Integrated Circuit industry and retired as an Application Engineer with Mentor Graphics, one of the largest Circuit Design Software companies in the country.

We were working and living together here and we took this opportunity to really get to know each other. The day I joined the Navy, Richard was only ten years old and as a teenager, I had very little interaction with someone so much younger. Now at this time in our lives, we were virtual strangers but a close kinship developed immediately. Over the years we would be accused of routinely dismissing anyone else present when we were together. For example, Richard and I took a visiting friend of mine to dinner and the poor guy later said he felt like he was there alone. I felt really bad about that but something happens when we are together that tends to exclude the rest of the world.

Now we are at the point where I decided I wanted to build a boat. Connie, who by now was an executive with an insurance company and not wanting to lose the security of her job and the house we had bought, elected to stay in Dallas. I regretted having to leave her but I was on a Holy Quest. This was something I really had to do. My only regret was that it took me so long to realize what it was I had been searching for all these years. I didn't realize it at the time but I was now on my way to finding what I had been subconsciously dreaming of from early childhood sitting high up in the limbs of our Elm tree.

# Epilogue

Looking back at my seventy four years I can only marvel at what incredible good luck followed me most of the time. I was just too young to be drafted in WW2 but I served during the Korean War. I was lucky to be in the Atlantic Theater and stayed as far from Korea as you can get. After leaving the Navy, I entered the work force at exactly the right time and the right place to get in at the very beginning of the Integrated Circuit Industry surge. This was a time of open opportunities just waiting to be grabbed. Even though I worked for many different companies, I would not have to actively look for a job for over thirty years. Even when in Hawaii, I was unable to escape being employed. Originally I had the only Printed Circuit Design position in the entire State and was lured all the way back from my South Pacific cruise to help them out. When I decided to build my boat, everything effortlessly just fell into place. Looking back I see all the doors that were open to me then are now closed. It is no longer possible for anyone to get a good high tech job with as little preparation as I had. The location I used to build my boat was turned into a wildlife sanctuary shortly after I left and all the remaining boats there were evicted. The Hawaiian anchorage I used for over a year in Pokai Bay was brought under the State Harbors control and can now be used for only three days at a time. The free anchorage in Keehi Lagoon was converted into a Harbors controlled mooring with buoy rentals only. The location in Waianae I used to rebuild my boat has been developed with new houses. Even my year in the Fiji Islands was fortuitous as shortly after I left, their government went to hell and they suffered several coups by the Army. The Hawaiian company which had me captive for so long, no longer exists. At moments of reflection when I find myself wishing I could do it all over again, I realize this could only happen once. I am saddened by the thought that everything that was open for me, is now gone.

There have been many times in History when there were plenty opportunities for the adventurous but at no other time in history would the living conditions be as good as they were when I needed them.

# Appendix A

The design method I used in building this boat was twofold. One was to make everything past center. Simply stated this means there are no flat surfaces or straight lines anywhere. The second is to make all joining elements have equal strength and modulus of elasticity. The first element creates a shape which is strong but light like an egg shell. The second spreads any flexing completely across a structure and eliminates "hinging" at weak spots. In order to accomplish both of these requirements, I built up the shape by using one half inch square redwood laths bent across an internal temporary frame. Each lath nailed to the preceding one for their full length kept the surface even and smooth minimizing the number of frames need to define the shape. Using this method, compound shapes can be fabricated. Finally on both the inside and outside surfaces, several laminations of polypropylene fabric with polyester or epoxy resins are applied with the warp and weft running at a forty five degree angle to the run of the lath. This results in every seam between the laths being crossed by one hundred percent of the cloth threads. This makes a very strong light sandwich which needs little permanent internal framing or support.

The actual construction of the final design was done in three stages. The first was constructing the basic saucer shape in two halves standing on their centers. Secondly after laying them down, I constructed the center hull on top of them which resulted in the structure now being upside down. Before I turned the thing over, I finished the application of cloth and resin on what was to be the top inside. Now I had to turn it over. After finishing all the laminations on the inside, I finally attached the two outer hulls. The entire structure was completely sealed against moisture and vermin with polypropylene cloth and polyester resin. The final finish on the outside was a lamination of cloth called Dynel. This is a short fiber highly abrasive resistant material which can be sanded into a nice smooth surface or left in its original fuzzy state making an excellent non skid surface.

An additional unique feature of the new design in Hawaii was the location of a Dagger Board eleven feet forward of the centerline and a Lee Board mounted ten feet astern of center. The Lee Board was clamped with a turnbuckle which set its angle of attack. Finally a wind vane controlled trim tab was mounted on the trailing edge of the Lee Board. In normal use, the Lee Board turnbuckle would be set to balance the rig so there would be little correction in steering needed. All the trim tab needed to do was add or subtract a bit to the work the Lee Board was doing in order to keep the boat on course. When running down wind, all boats have a strong tendency to broach which means they want turn and lay sideways to the waves. This tenancy requires a lot of rudder correction to keep the boat on a straight course. This system of mine prevented this broaching by shifting the center of lateral resistance or pivot point, far to the rear when the Dagger Board in the front was raised. However when sailing up wind with the Dagger Board down, the twenty four foot separation between the two points of lateral resistance made the boat sail like it was on a track. The total system worked so well, I could always steer the boat when under power using only the four inch long trim tab extension. The final tweak was the installation of a canard wing on each side of the trim tab which created a balanced trim tab reducing the effort needed from the wind vane.

Laminating cloth on half section

View up inside half section

Ready to come into the light

All together    Lift!

I have a host of friends

If there's a will, there is a way

Almost half way up

Half way down

Ready for next phase

Finally ready to launch

View of cockpit

Hanging out in Santa Cruz

Hanging out in Kailua Kona

Author with crazy halfbeak fish

Redesigned boat in Waianae

Hauling out at Keehi

Author and Wendy at galley table

Hippy Author